THE KIMBERLEY

AUSTRALIA'S UNIQUE NORTH-WEST

Lake Argyle at the Ord Dam

THE
KIMBERLEY

AUSTRALIA'S UNIQUE NORTH-WEST

JOCELYN BURT

with poems by Neroli Roberts

TUART
HOUSE

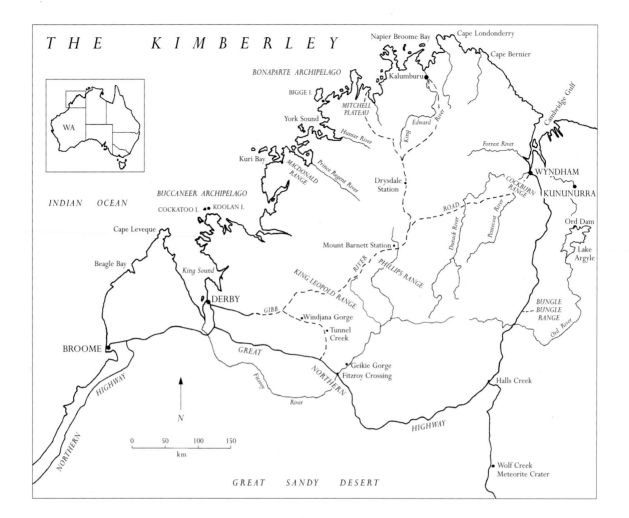

THE KIMBERLEY

ACKNOWLEDGMENTS

I am indebted to many people in the Kimberley for their help
in the preparation of this book. In particular I wish to thank
Jack and Neroli Roberts, Kununurra; Bob and Heather Taylor,
Kununurra; Errol and Maxine Snow, Wyndham; Ian and Sue
Sinnamon, Home Valley Station, east Kimberley; Sid and Pat
Sharp, Lake Argyle Village; Graeme Macarthur ('The
General'), Halls Creek and Bungle Bungle Tours; Kingfisher
Aviation, Halls Creek; Safari-Trek Australia, Perth and
Kununurra; Kings Park and Botanic Garden, Perth;
Department of Conservation and Land Management, Western
Australia; Kimberley Explorer Cruises Pty Ltd, Broome, and
Captain Arie Nygh and crew of the *Kimberley Explorer* for one
of the most memorable voyages of my life. Finally, I would like
to express my gratitude to Dame Mary Durack, for agreeing
to write the Foreword to this book.

Earlier versions of some of the poems that appear in this book
were first published in *Artlook*, the *Brumby*, and the *Kimberley
Echo*.

Most of the photographs in the book were taken with a
Mamiya RB67 camera.

This edition published 1996 by
University of Western Australia Press
Nedlands, Western Australia 6907
under the Tuart House imprint

First published in 1989 by
Houghton Mifflin Australia Pty Ltd, reprinted 1990.

Copyright © Jocelyn Burt 1996

National Library of Australia
Cataloguing in Publications entry:

Burt, Jocelyn
    The Kimberley: Australia's unique north-west.

    {Rev. ed.}.
    ISBN 1 875560 78 5.

    1. Kimberley (W.A.) – Description and travel. 2. Kimberley
    (W.A.) – Pictorial works. 3. Kimberley (W.A.) – Poetry.
    I. Roberts, Neroli. II. Title.

919.414

Front cover image: Pentecost River and Cockburn Range
Back cover image: Boab tree near Derby

Edited by Alex Skovron
Designed by Noni Edmunds
Cover design by Robyn Mundy, Mundy Design, Perth
Typeset in Perpetua by Setrite, Hong Kong
Printed by South China Printing Co (1988) Ltd, Hong Kong

CONTENTS

The Sleeping Buddha, Lake Kununurra

*F*OREWORD

As always when returning to the country of my earliest memories, the visit provided by this book has been for me a heartwarming experience.

Jocelyn Burt, her keen-eyed camera readily to hand, converses with her readers as fellow-travellers while conveying them by various means of transport around the coast and throughout the inland of this vast area. We explore the unique vegetation of the Mitchell Plateau and venture into the Bungle Bungle Range, 'discovered' not long ago. We wonder at the grandeur and variety of the landscape as we proceed — the flat-topped ranges and jagged cliffs outlined against the sky, the rivers, gorges and lily-covered lagoons. From a respectful distance we see saltwater crocodiles on riverbanks, while at closer quarters wallabies and kangaroos pause to observe us enquiringly. Not so the many varieties of birdlife, from bright-feathered twittering finches, noisy parrots, cockatoos and whistling ducks to the stately brolga and jabiru.

Our tour leader, giving us the basic facts of history along the way, takes us to the ports of Broome, Derby and Wyndham, established in the 1880s for the pearlers and pastoralists and the influx of prospectors to the goldrush at Halls Creek. At Broome we board a luxurious catamaran for a thirteen-day cruise north around the lonely coast and outlying islands discovered by pioneer navigators of centuries past. From Wyndham we make our way inland to Kununurra, a town created on the Ord River in the 1960s when confidence in the future of a major crop-growing industry spurred the construction of the largest artificial lake in Australia. The land that lies beneath these waters was the greater part of Argyle Station, taken up by my grandfather as a result of Alexander Forrest's encouraging report of 1879. As Forrest had foreseen, the country proved reliable enough to sustain its sheep and cattle properties, while indications of various mineral deposits led to recurrent waves of excited speculation. It was not until recent years, however, that the discovery of diamonds brought increased prosperity to the east Kimberley and Kununurra, which had declined with the disappointing outcome of agricultural experiments.

Neroli Roberts, a long-term resident of the area whose poems are interspersed throughout the book, has acquired a close affinity with the country and its people. She has a strong feeling for the timeless quality of the land and the Dreamtime spell of its creator spirits, of which evidence survives on rockfaces and in obscure caves. Some retain the ochre-outlined imprints of human hands, and Neroli sees one such hand as that of a 'Dark sister without name or face': she presses her palm against it, 'in Greeting'. Then again, both Neroli and Jocelyn write of the elephantine, often grotesque Kimberley boab trees as an outstanding feature of the landscape; the poet sees the boabs as friendly individuals, 'part of the Infinite Whole'. . .

This book, having taken us to what the author regards as one of the most exciting and awe-inspiring regions of Australia, should make more widely known the fact that the remote 'Never-Never' of former times is today accessible to all. I wish the reader 'happy travelling'.

Mary Durack

Rocks near the jetty at Roebuck Bay

INTRODUCING THE KIMBERLEY

> If one were to paint this country in its true colours, I doubt it would be believed. It would be said at least that the artist exaggerated greatly, for never have I seen such richness and variety of hue as in these ranges and in the vivid flowers of this northern spring.
>
> MICHAEL DURACK, 1882 (quoted in *Kings in Grass Castles* by Mary Durack)

IT IS hardly surprising that many people consider the Kimberley to be one of the most exciting places in Australia. Indeed, those who know it intimately may tell you that no other area on the continent can match its beauty and its grandeur.

One of the earth's wildest regions, the Kimberley is a world of worn and colourful ranges, spectacular gorges, vast plains, strange boab trees, lush waterholes, and great rivers that flow only for a few months of the year. Its rugged landscapes stretch the mind and evoke in the traveller a tremendous sense of awe. Somehow one has here a heightened expectation of adventure, largely because this inhospitable yet stunningly beautiful region is still very much 'last frontier' country. It is a place ideal for keeping secrets, and the chance that undiscovered scenic treasures may lie hidden in its remote and inaccessible areas has captivated the public's imagination; certainly few places have stirred such interest in recent times as the 'discovery' in 1983 of the Bungle Bungle Range in the east Kimberley. As it is, some of the region's grandest sights — mostly unknown to the world — are seen by relatively few people.

The Kimberley covers the vast north-west corner of Australia. Geographically, it is the part of the continent closest to Indonesia, which lies less than 500 kilometres to the north. Nearly twice the size of the state of Victoria, it is bound by the Northern Territory to the east and the desolate Great Sandy Desert to the south, and its shores are washed by the Indian Ocean and the Timor Sea. Much of its north and central area is dominated by a series of plateaux and ranges, which gradually give way to extensive floodplains and gently undulating sandy country.

It may seem a long journey from anywhere to reach the Kimberley — its northernmost town, Wyndham, lies about 3200 kilometres by road from Perth, and some 1050 kilometres separate Broome in the west and Kununurra in the east — but thanks to improved roads and air-services the region is not as isolated as it used to be. Distances don't worry the locals, who think nothing of flying from Kununurra to Darwin for a weekend, or driving 100 kilometres from Wyndham to Kununurra for a weekly game of golf; visitors too, in their eagerness to explore the area, are becoming less concerned with distance. All the Kimberley towns are linked by bitumen, and since the sealing of the last section of the Great Northern Highway that links Perth to the north-west, the number of tourists has grown from a steady flow in the 1970s to a flood in the 1980s.

There are only two seasons, the Wet (summer) and the Dry (winter). However, the weather here is subject to greater fluctuations than in the rest of tropical Australia: the monsoonal rains fall over a slightly shorter period, between December and March; and temperatures are higher in summer and lower in winter — in July it is not uncommon for the nights to drop to 0°C in some places. The best months for travelling are between May and September, the coolest time being from mid-June to the end of July, when the day temperatures are in the pleasant high-twenties. Much potential enjoyment is lost if campers choose to be in the Kimberley's inland regions between the end of September and the Wet, when temperatures can climb to well over 40°C for days on end; because of the effects this heat has on people, the time prior to the Wet is known as the 'troppo' or 'suicide' season. During the Dry, motorists in conventional cars can visit most of the popular scenic attractions, and for those who do not have suitable vehicles for places that are accessible only by four-wheel-drive, local commercial tours are available.

For me, the Kimberley is a very special place. Nowhere else in Australia have I been so aware of the sheer impact of colour in the landscapes. I marvel at the number of beautiful gorges throughout the region, and one of the joys of exploring them is that each is so different from the next — and the last one visited is always the best. Over the years I have made many trips to the Kimberley, mostly travelling in a conventional campervan, to discover places I hadn't been to before (there is never enough time to see everything in one visit) and to revisit old favourites; in the familiar places, I have often been rewarded by an even deeper awareness of beauty. Much of the Kimberley remains a mystery to the outside world, and there is still a great deal to learn. Most people outside the West — including the eastern states' media — don't even get the name right: Western Australians will firmly tell you it is 'the Kimberley', *not* the plural form 'Kimberleys'.

In this book, through photographs and the recounting of some of my experiences, and with Neroli Roberts's delightful poems, I hope to give the reader — and the prospective traveller — an idea of what there is to see in the Kimberley, and to convey something of its marvellous beauty and character. For those who have already been, I hope many pleasant memories will be refreshed, and a better understanding gained of a region that I firmly believe to be the most exciting in Australia.

Jocelyn Burt

Piccaninny Gorge, Bungle Bungle Range

Argyle Downs homestead

*E*ARLY DAYS

LONG before any exploration by land, seafarers had made contact with the Kimberley coast. The first Europeans were possibly the Portuguese prior to 1600, followed by the Dutch navigator Abel Tasman in 1644. The English buccaneer William Dampier visited the coast in 1688, then again in 1699 in the *Roebuck*. The French followed about a century later, and although Nicolas Baudin's survey in 1801 was brief, much of his nomenclature remains on maps today. Phillip Parker King, son of the New South Wales governor, completed an outline of the north-west coast in a series of voyages between 1818 and 1821, and discovered the Prince Regent River, describing it as one of the most remarkable features of the region. However, the coast was not mapped properly until 1838, when John Wickham and John Lort Stokes in the *Beagle* explored it during a five-year survey of the northern shores. That same year, George Grey made the first land expedition. In an attempt to blaze a trail from the north to Perth, he landed with fourteen men at Hanover Bay and managed to cross the rugged Macdonald Range; but he travelled little further than the Glenelg River, as he was wounded during a skirmish with Aborigines. He was the first European to record the spectacular Wandjina cave paintings: the huge figures draped in long robes and with heads encircled by halo-like rays. Grey's favourable report on Camden Sound and its agricultural possibilities led to the ill-fated first attempt to settle the Kimberley in 1865.

The most important expedition, and one that ultimately opened the Kimberley to permanent settlers, was led by Alexander Forrest in 1879. With a party of eight, Forrest travelled from Beagle Bay to Darwin. He followed the Fitzroy River and at Fitzroy Crossing made an arduous detour to Collier Bay, discovering on the way the Oscar and King Leopold ranges; in the east Kimberley he reported good grassland for stock, and discovered the Ord River. Two years later the Murray Squatting Company leased a vast tract of land for a sheep-station near Beagle Bay, and shortly afterwards other pastoralists followed. Between 1882 and 1885 the east Kimberley was settled by cattlemen from eastern parts of Australia who overlanded their stock in epic treks across the continent; among these remarkable pioneers were the Duracks. In the 1970s one of the Duracks' stations, 'Argyle Downs', was submerged by Lake Argyle, part of the Ord River Scheme, but the historic homestead was moved to high ground near the present Lake Argyle Village.

The discovery of gold at Halls Creek in the early 1880s drew thousands of people to the Kimberley. Derby was settled in 1883, and in 1886 Wyndham was established to serve the needs of the growing pastoral industry; Broome was declared a town in 1883, and soon became the centre for pearling activities. The Kimberley was named in the 1880s after the British Colonial Secretary, the Earl of Kimberley.

Cambridge Gulf, from the Five Rivers Lookout, Wyndham

THE COASTAL TOWNS

SOME people claim that many towns in Australia are so similar in appearance that in seeing one you have seen them all. Well, nothing could be further from the truth when it comes to the Kimberley's three coastal towns: Broome, Derby and Wyndham.

Of the three, Broome is the largest, with a permanent population of around 6000 and swelling to thousands more during the winter months. Situated on a finger of land that separates the wide expanse of Roebuck Bay from the Indian Ocean, the town is also the western gateway to the Kimberley. A growing number of visitors from all states and overseas have discovered it to be a wonderful holiday haven, and for Western Australians it has become the Cairns of the West: each winter thousands head for this warm spot in order to escape the lower temperatures of the south. Broome also has the most pleasant climate in the Kimberley, being cooler than inland regions.

One of Broome's many drawcards is Cable Beach — 'the best in the West,' the locals will tell you. Lying on the ocean side of the town and bordered by dunes varying in colour from white to red, this splendid beach is a good 150 metres wide from dunes to sea at an average low tide. For me, the incredible spaciousness of Cable Beach epitomizes the essential and precious freedom that Australia offers so widely, and whenever I run along the water's edge in the soft beauty of dawn or dusk, my spirit rejoices in the vast stretch of sand that sweeps for 22 kilometres to the distant horizon. The gentle surf provides safe swimming — unlike the waters of Roebuck Bay, which are full of sharks.

Roebuck Bay may be unsuitable for swimming but it is stunning in its colour, and on every visit to Broome I spend hours there with the camera. At the jetty end of the beach a heap of weirdly shaped red rocks engraved by weathering with swirling patterns gives way to a series of red dunes and a beach of red sand; this, together with the brilliant turquoise sea washing the red beach, gives the place an extraordinary atmosphere. On a recent visit to the beach I found that a huge shed had been erected close to one of my favourite photographic spots among the rocks. Alarmed, I asked a workman at the shed if there were any plans to develop the rocky area. 'No, we're not allowed to touch the rocks,' he said reassuringly.

At Gantheaume Point, at the end of Cable Beach, there is more vivid colour as a profusion of red rocks sprawls into the sea. An unlikely treasure lies underwater here in the form of a dinosaur's footprints set in rock about 30 metres out to sea from the point. During the low September king-tides one year, I had, not very enthusiastically, joined a number of keen searchers in a perilous scramble over the grey, slimy rocks to find these prehistoric tracks. However, the slippery mud had a somewhat dampening effect on our spirits and most of us gave up long before reaching our goal; those who did reach the area couldn't find the elusive footprints anyway. Instead everybody had to be content with the replicas pressed in a slab of concrete at the carpark.

Climate and coast aside, Broome is renowned for its oriental character and charm, attributed to the strong Asian influence it has retained from the great pearling days. By 1910 Broome, known as the 'Port of Pearls', was the leading pearl centre in the world with a fleet of more than 350 luggers, many of whose crewmen were Japanese, Malays or Javanese. The pearling industry began its decline soon after 1914, but the demand for cultured pearls prevented Broome from becoming a ghost-town; in 1956 a pearl farm was established at Kuri Bay and luggers from Broome began fishing for live shells to be 'seeded'. Lying north of the Buccaneer Archipelago, the Kuri Bay farm continues to produce the highest-quality cultured pearls in the world, and at a very fast rate: here it takes eighteen months to two years for a pearl to grow, whereas elsewhere it takes up to three years. This is because the Kimberley coast's water is particularly rich in nutrients brought in by the big tides; it is also very clean.

Broome's annual festival is aptly called Shintu Matsuri — Festival of the Pearl — and is held for ten days every August–September. It was more by accident than design that I attended it one year. Having no idea that the festival was on, I arrived in town with friends. The past few weeks had been spent in the bush and we were looking forward to some civilized accommodation, but to our dismay we had trouble finding it; we also didn't relish a Broome seething with people. However, it turned out to be a great week, full of interesting activities and sights — including the magical moonrise known as the 'Golden Staircase to the Moon'.

In recent years the town has undergone many changes in order to cater for the fast-growing tourist industry, and during winter months you would almost think there was a permanent Shintu festival in progress, so crowded is the town with visitors. One area that has been developed extensively is the Cable Beach Road, and on my last visit I was saddened to see that the popular

Gantheaume Point

caravan park situated opposite the beach had been moved back a block to provide space for an upmarket accommodation complex. However, despite the changes that have left many people grumbling, Broome is still Broome, with a special atmosphere that will never entirely be lost. You can still get some of the best Chinese food in the West there; indeed, the standard of cuisine throughout the town has improved remarkably in recent years. I can't help feeling that most visitors to Broome will, on arrival, virtually forget that any other world exists: Broome is still that sort of place.

The coast north of Broome is worth exploring, though a four-wheel-drive vehicle is recommended. 'The main road up the coast is all right if you don't mind corrugations that will shake your car to bits,' one local cheerfully told me. He further explained that the tracks off to Willie Creek, Quondong and Barred Creek (where the Petrified Forest is found) were very boggy because the area is tidal. I decided to leave the van behind and take a day-tour to Manari, 100 kilometres up the coast. It was a good trip and I have lasting memories of the incredibly red cliffs at James Price Point, and of Manari's vast area of exposed oyster-covered reef as well as the long sandy beach with its astonishing assortment of shells washed up by the last tide.

Derby lies 232 kilometres north-east of Broome. With a population of more than 3000, it is the second-largest town in the Kimberley and serves as an administrative centre for the west Kimberley district; it is also the gateway for tourists heading for the region's many spectacular gorges. Since Derby is situated in the heart of boab-tree country, it is not surprising to find that many grand old boabs line the streets and grace the gardens, giving the town an unusual but distinctly 'Kimberley' atmosphere. Its shops and facilities are scattered all over the place, but this doesn't seem to worry the locals — they show much more affection for this town than do the tourists, who tend to regard it merely as a necessary stop for petrol and provisions.

Once, I decided to see what Derby looked like from the air. To my astonishment the flight revealed an unusual beauty in the mudflats around the town, a beauty that at ground-level would have been impossible to see. In the vast areas of mud that blanketed the coastal plains between the mangrove swamps, tidal erosion had fashioned in the soft ground a fantastic display of designs resembling trees and ferns. Many eroded areas were filling with the incoming tide, and when the sun momentarily glinted on the water the patterns seemed to flood with liquid silver and the world below glittered in a breathtaking display. The detail and harmony of the 'branches' were exquisite. Someone later told me that he had attempted to find the elusive tree-patterns in the mudflats, but had managed only to flounder for a few metres in the soft and rather smelly mud; he was also nearly eaten alive by hungry insects.

Wyndham is the east Kimberley's only coastal town and lies towards the end of Cambridge Gulf on the north coast. The town is in two sections, Wyndham and Port Wyndham, and has a population of around 1300. In the 1980s the Port was given a new lease of life with an increase of shipping that carried out ore containing zinc, lead and copper, and transported live cattle to countries in the Far East. Over the years some rather crude statements have been made about Wyndham, which has gained a reputation of being a bit of a dump. Certainly it isn't the best place to be before the Wet starts, when temperatures climb well into the stifling forties and the town is smothered in a heat-haze so dense that you feel you can scoop it in your hands. But Wyndham has character. A little time is needed to discover it, and the more I visit the place the more I like it. For one thing, it has the Kimberley's shadiest caravan park — and that is a real blessing in the hot north.

A number of historic sites and buildings are to be found around the town, especially in the Port area. One quaint old building that now houses a souvenir shop has become quite a tourist attraction: Honest John's, run by 'Honest John' himself (yes, that's the name he is known by). Someone suggested I should have a talk with him, as he liked tourists. The shop was easy enough to find in the Port's main street. Among an incredible array of exotic T-shirts, Aboriginal artefacts and the host of other goods that filled the shop, I was greeted by a sturdily built man with a good mop of hair tinged with grey and a great bushy black beard that could not entirely hide his strong features and piercing grey eyes. I asked him how he had come by the name 'Honest John'. 'Well, my name is John,' he chuckled with a wicked twinkle in his eyes, 'and I've always been known as a bit of a rogue.' Rogue or not, Honest John is good value. This colourful character, who for years drove trucks for the meatworks until it closed down in 1986, knows the district well and is a veritable mine of information.

Next to Honest John's shop was his Tea Gardens (where you could buy an Honest Burger), and by the garden tables a large ornamental crocodile rested on the grass. As I discovered while talking with Honest John, Wyndham is very crocodile-minded, which is hardly surprising as there are plenty around Cambridge Gulf — and these are the dangerous saltwater species, known throughout the north as 'salties'. For years they were attracted into the Wyndham area by the local meatworks, which flushed its waste-matter of blood and scrap-meat into the Gulf. The meatworks closed down, but the Crocodile Lookout is still at the spot where the waste once escaped, and today you may see the odd croc basking on the mud nearby. If you miss seeing a live one, there is 'The Big Crocodile' that stands larger than life on the lawns outside the post office. A local resident so loves the critters that he keeps them as pets in his backyard; his largest is a 5.4 metre salty which many years ago regularly came out of the mangroves at night to roam the Port's main street and terrify the locals when they left the pub at closing-time. The crocodile-lover offered to capture it in return for a permit to keep the reptile. Understandably, the permit was issued at once.

In many ways Wyndham is not like the average country town. Take the local gaol, for instance, set in the middle of the Port's main street. One morning I noticed that the gates were wide open, and about a dozen inmates lolled about on the lawns; a notice near the entrance advised that trespassers would be prosecuted. 'Surely some of the prisoners escape!' I exclaimed to a local councillor. 'Where would they go?' he replied. 'They would soon be picked up in this country, and anyway, they get three good meals a day and a heap of videos to watch.' In a classic piece of understatement he added, 'It's not a maximum-security prison, you know.'

Beyond the town itself there is some magnificent scenery. Wyndham nestles at the foot of a range called The Bastion, and from its summit the Five Rivers Lookout gives excellent views over Cambridge Gulf. Seen from this high vantage-point the landscapes are forbidding, and the empty mud and salt flats, broken near the coast by a network of meandering watercourses lined with mangroves, take on a new dimension of vastness and isolation which is quite awesome. I prefer to visit the lookout in the late afternoon, when the sun casts a sparkling glow on the Gulf's waters, and the surrounding countryside is bathed in delicate pinks and blues that give an uncharacteristic softness to the barren hills and plains. A trip to Wyndham would be worthwhile for this alone.

There is more beauty at Parry Lagoon Reserve (originally Marlgu Bird Sanctuary), off the Kununurra road, about 16 kilometres south of the town. A new road to the lagoon has been built and passes over the hill where the old telegraph station once stood; but many people still prefer the old road that crosses the floodplains. If you go the old way it is wise to stay on the firm main track, as there are some nasty patches of soft talc-like bulldust lying elsewhere. The reserve is a place where birdlovers can happily spend hours watching the many different species that flock to this oasis-like long narrow lagoon, which has permanent water throughout most of the dry season.

Parry Lagoon Reserve

An aerial view of Derby. Situated at the southern end of King Sound, the town is edged by extensive mudflats that are exposed at low tide. This coast has some of the biggest tides in the world.

A tidal erosion pattern at Derby is flooded with liquid silver as the sun glints in the water trapped in the erosions at low tide.

Facing page:

Sunset over Cambridge Gulf at Port Wyndham. About 85 percent of Western Australia's fresh water pours into Cambridge Gulf from five rivers: the Pentecost, the Ord, the Durack, the Forrest and the King.

Saltwater or estuarine crocodile (*Crocodylus porosus*), at Wyndham. Australia's two species of crocodile — the dangerous 'salty' and the harmless Johnstone's freshwater — are protected by law.

Pearling luggers moored at high tide
in Broome — a sight rarely seen
these days, as luggers no longer
operate out of the town.

An active Chinese dragon leads the
parade held during Shintu Matsuri,
Broome's annual Festival of the Pearl.

The 'Golden Staircase to the Moon' is
a phenomenon that occurs only a few
times a year when the full moon rises
over Roebuck Bay during a low king-
tide. As the moonlight reflects in the
pools of water left on the ocean bed
it creates the effect of steps.

Facing page:

In places, red dunes give way to fine
white sand at Cable Beach, Broome.

Filled with water after a brief shower,
one of the concrete replicas of a
dinosaur's footprints shines in the sun
at Gantheaume Point.

Waterlilies, Parry Lagoon, near Wyndham

Panorama

Life to me
in the Kimberley
is here and now
— a passing shower
— a tree
— a flower
destined to bloom
for one brief hour
and then, make room
for others.

But some
with clearer eyes can see
— the passing shower
— the flower
— the tree
in the panorama of Eternity.

NEROLI ROBERTS

Cliffs, King George River

KIMBERLEY COAST: A VOYAGE

AS THE birds fly, the Kimberley coast spans well over 1000 kilometres, but if all the inlets and bays were measured it would probably be twice that distance. Seen from the air, this indented coastline seems even more broken than the map suggests. Lying crumpled and creased, its shores are notched with a myriad mangroved estuaries, bays and sandy beaches; plunging cliffs and rocky masses from the great northern plateau push boldly into the sea, and craggy headlands like arthritic fingers point crookedly towards stony islands and innumerable hidden reefs that litter the offshore waters. Its tides are among some of the biggest in the world, and in places they are treacherously strong and unpredictable — serving notice that access to this land where few roads penetrate may be difficult, and dangerous.

After flying over the area between Derby and Cockatoo Island, I longed to see it from the sea and to discover some of its well-guarded secrets. At first this seemed impossible, for who ventured into these remote waters? Then I heard about the *Kimberley Explorer,* a luxury 34-metre catamaran that in the dry season ran regular trips for those interested in exploring the coast between Broome and Derby. It sounded like sheer adventure, an ideal way to discover this coast.

I joined the *Kimberley Explorer* in Broome. Over the following thirteen days we explored bays, inlets, caves, islands, rivers and tributaries that had rarely been visited by Europeans; we called in to places of great historic importance, and to some that hadn't even been named. Wildlife abounded, and there was a continuous feast of superb scenery. Every day we made at least one shore excursion. Although the *Kimberley Explorer* regularly visited certain places on every trip, the captain, Arie Nygh, explained at the start that each voyage was different because tides governed access to various spots. Except for a few key locations there were no tide-charts, and those available were not relevant for elsewhere; the skipper's local knowledge of the tides' peculiarities was essential.

Our first excursion was to the Lacepede Islands, situated about 30 kilometres west of Beagle Bay. In the nineteenth century these remote islands were the centre of an extraordinary international incident concerning their potentially wealthy metre-deep guano fertilizer deposits. For a short spell in 1876 the Stars and Stripes flew over the place, raised by a Yankee adventurer claiming possession for his country because the islands lay outside Australia's then 12-mile offshore limit. When an Australian mining company started to remove the guano, the American consul in Melbourne requested that Washington send a warship to the islands 'to safeguard American property'!

Now an important restricted wildlife reserve, the Lacepedes' three sparsely vegetated low islands are a major nesting-ground for a host of lesser frigatebirds, brown boobies and sooty terns, as well as for green turtles. It would be easy for visitors to cause havoc among the nesting-sites, because when the scared parent birds fly off, the unattended eggs and young chicks are in grave danger of being seized by the ever-hungry gulls; for this reason we were asked not to walk through the rookeries. As it turned out, there was excellent viewing from the beach — and so much of interest that it was hard to decide what to photograph first. Turtle tracks were everywhere; the sky was full of birds; brown boobies sat broodily on nests close to the beach, their appealingly ugly larger chicks, so fluffy that they appeared as big as their parents, glaring at us and squawking crossly. Just as I was about to photograph two notably handsome Mum and Dad boobies with their young, someone called out, 'Come and see the turtles!' Several young green turtles were swimming close to the shore.

About 3000 islands lie off the Kimberley coast. More than 800 of them comprise the Buccaneer Archipelago, which contains the richest iron-ore deposits in the world (it is said that the ore here is of such a high grade that two rocks can be welded together). Two of these islands are renowned for their mines: Cockatoo and Koolan. After 32 years of mining, Cockatoo closed in 1986, and before long there was talk of turning the island into a tourist resort; Koolan expects to be mining well into the 1990s. Although we didn't land on the islands (Koolan, with its 900 workers, is a closed BHP town), we were able to have a close look at the open-cut mines from the boat.

Our shore excursion here was to a rockpool in Crocodile Creek, situated on the mainland near Koolan Island. The pool, fed by a waterfall, lay a short distance upstream at the top of a high rocky wall. At high tide the creek water comes to the top of the wall, providing easy access to the

Crocodile Creek

pool; to overcome the difficulty of getting there at low tide, the Koolan folk have erected a nine-metre steel ladder at the wall to enable them to climb up to the barbecue area they had built by the pool. During big spring-tides the incoming water actually flows over the wall and fills the pool, allowing a boat to reach the waterfall — but if the boat doesn't leave before that tide drops, its skipper might have to wait about three months for the next big one to float it over the wall. Fortunately it was a normal high tide when we arrived, as it wouldn't have been much fun lugging the food-laden eskies up the ladder. While the prawns and barramundi steaks sizzled over the fire, we swam in the pool.

It was the morning after leaving Buccaneer Archipelago that we sighted the humpback whales. Breakfast turned into a rather disrupted affair as everybody raced up to the deck to spot them; but they were elusive, surfacing only at odd intervals, and then you had to be quick to spot one. After breakfast I returned to my cabin and, not even thinking of whales, pulled up the blinds — to be presented with the wonderful spectacle of a mother and baby surfacing only metres from the window. Entranced, I watched their sleek black shapes arch slowly through the water as they slipped into the silvery path of light cast on the sea by the early-morning sun. Just before they disappeared the baby did what all whales are expected to do: it blew out a spout of water.

Later I sat on the top deck to see if any more were around. The sea was calm, with glassy smooth patches lying among the soft ripples that served as waves; in the distance a line of rose-coloured cliffs separated the smooth sea from the blue sky, which was empty except for a row of small cottonwool clouds that hung suspended just above the horizon. I saw no more whales, but the simplicity of the scene and the gloriously soft colours were a balm — indeed a tonic — for the spirit.

At Llangi, a sacred Aboriginal site known to only a few Europeans, we stopped to see some quite startling rock formations known as the 'Petrified Warriors', after the warriors who, in Aboriginal mythology, took part in a big Dreamtime battle here between the Wandjina and other spirits. Lining the shore at one end of the attractive cove was a veritable army of weirdly eroded, slender sandstone rocks that rose many metres in height. Like sentinels, they guarded the nearby entrance to Llangi Gorge, a small but scenic gorge lined with block-like rocks.

Near Kuri Bay lay Camden Harbour, the site of a disastrous scheme to colonize the area in the mid-1860s. Some time earlier the explorers Stokes and Grey had reported seeing fine pastureland here, and consequently many families with their stock migrated from New South Wales. Eight months after landing, most of the cattle had died and the settlers were struggling for survival in a virtually uninhabitable land; shortly afterwards the government ordered the remaining families to leave. Today, one of the few reminders of this fiasco lies on a small island in the harbour: the grave of one of the young settlers, Mary Pascoe, who died in childbirth. We made a brief stop to see this lonely grave that rested by an old boab tree covered in unreadable carvings made by the early settlers.

One historic carving left last century on a boab tree has remained remarkably clear. At Careening Bay, off York Sound, a sturdy, double-trunked boab bears the inscription HMC MERMAID 1820. This was done by the ship's crew while repairs were made to the cutter during Phillip Parker King's first voyage to the region. The boab was rediscovered in 1973, when a Western Australian government expedition to the north-west coast searched for the tree because King had mentioned it in his journal. It was very early morning when we landed at Careening Bay. Before inspecting the boab I relived a little history when one of the passengers, an antique-dealer from Melbourne who had memorized the drawing of the ship's camp made by the crew's artist, was able to locate the exact site.

The Prince Regent Reserve was one of the highlights of the voyage. Lying off Brunswick Bay and covering more than 6000 square kilometres, the reserve is one of the world's most undisturbed nature sanctuaries. Little has changed in the area since the first Europeans visited. A major feature is the majestic Prince Regent River, which has cut an enormous straight gorge through the region's rugged sandstone plateau before emptying into the spacious, almost landlocked St George Basin. From the moment the *Kimberley Explorer* entered the Basin the scenery was interesting: the distinctive shapes of Mount Trafalgar and Mount Waterloo dominated the landscape, and in places high pinky-orange cliffs, their reflections beautifully shimmering, edged the calm water of the bay.

For about 75 kilometres upstream the Prince Regent River is navigable, but maps warn that great care should be taken because of the numerous rocks present — including uncharted ones that may exist. With the *Kimberley Explorer*'s good shallow draught we had no trouble reaching Kings Cascades, situated in an inlet off the river. At the cascades a small waterfall tumbled about 30 metres down great steps of chunky black basalt rock decorated with vegetation that hung like long tresses of green hair. Nearby, curtains of frothing ferns and other plants clung to the rocky walls that flanked the cascades; these beautiful hanging gardens appeared to be fed by a constant seepage of moisture that dripped through the luxuriant growth like gentle rain. It was hard to believe that this glorious spot had recently been the scene of terrible tragedy: a young American woman on a private cruise had been taken by a crocodile while swimming here. Throughout the trip our crew was very strict as to where we swam, and a comprehensive lecture on crocodiles had been given earlier to inform everybody about their habits — and capabilities.

Although the Prince Regent River is a grand sight with its precipitous walls of jumbled King Leopold sandstone, the river's real beauty lies in its smaller and more sheltered tributaries and inlets. Fortunately we were able to explore some of them in the dinghies, and on land by foot. Once the main river was left behind it was like entering another world — a more intimate one, where details were easily observed in rocky outcrops, mangroves and other trees that reflected deeply in the narrow waterways. And when the boat's motor was turned off, it was a joy to listen to the natural sounds that broke the silence of the bush: the birdcalls, the sounds of insects, and the gentle lapping of the water through the mangroves.

North of Prince Regent Reserve lies the great Prince Frederick Harbour. Some spectacular rivers enter its waters, and it was from the mouth of the Hunter River that we explored the area. It is believed to have one of the largest populations of saltwater crocodiles in Australia, so we naturally expected to see plenty. Surprisingly, there were very few around. The *Kimberley Explorer*'s crew suspected they were being taken by poachers, because on recent trips the few that had been spotted behaved as if they had experienced being shot at. Crocodile skins fetch high prices whether or not they are legally obtained — and if ever a coast was open to poaching it is this one.

Towards sunset we went up the Hunter River in dinghies to look for crocodiles. I was thrilled more by the scenery than by the croc-spotting. The setting sun lit the great rugged cliffs that lined the river, and in the stillness of the evening the glowing walls mirrored in the water, spilling rich colour over its surface. The tide was on the way out, leaving great banks of mud exposed on both sides; the three small crocodiles we sighted had left deep slide-marks on the banks, which showed how soft the mud was here. A couple of times our dinghy's engine gave a sickening whine as it nearly caught in the mud, warning us that it was time to return to the boat. A night spent stuck fast in the river's bottom while waiting for the tide to turn had little appeal, especially as it was now quite cold on the water. By the time we got back we were all shivering. Stupidly, nobody had thought of taking jackets.

In the Bonaparte Archipelago we stopped at Bigge Island to see what must be some of the most striking cave paintings in the Kimberley. The paintings in the first cave depicted pipe-smoking figures wearing strange hats — possibly a record of the seventeenth-century Dutch explorers' visits to this coast — but it was the two huge nautical Wandjinas on the walls of the next cave which astonished us. Considerable mystery surrounds the Wandjina paintings that are found throughout the Kimberley. Although for generations the Aborigines have ritually touched up these strange mouthless figures wearing haloes, they were not the original artists. Local legends say the Wandjinas were Dreamtime supermen who came from the north and west, and on their death they assumed the form of rock paintings. The intriguing nautical versions of the Wandjinas known as Kaiaras, depicted in local mythology as weather gods, are also said to have come from over the sea. Because of the paintings' similarity to ancient art in the Middle East, theories abound as to whether Egyptian or Phoenician sailors may have visited this north-west coast, perhaps blown off course by the north-west monsoons. There is even an odd rumour that the wreck of an ancient sailing-galley lies buried in the mud somewhere along this shore! So far the region's isolation has been the paintings' best protection — though there are also some unusual and stern custodians: two large resident saltwater crocodiles guard the beach that provides access to the caves, and this makes a landing possible only when they are not around.

Kings Cascades, Prince Regent River

After we had attended a corroboree at the Aboriginal settlement of Kalumburu, the *Kimberley Explorer* headed towards a place I believe to be one of the most visually stunning in Australia: the King George River. Lying west of Cape Bernier on the far north coast, the King George's estuary hides in a section of coast bound by high rugged sandstone cliffs that promise plenty of good scenery beyond. The river too is flanked by great rocky walls that become steadily higher as it narrows. After travelling about 12 kilometres we reached the end of the gorge, where in two places thundering waterfalls normally poured down to the river; on this occasion, however, we were presented with only a trickle because the Wet had been unusually light. But even without the waterfalls this section of the river was magnificent. In crevasses and narrow gorges — little more than great clefts in the rocky wall that rarely if ever saw sunlight — a mass of ferns flourished, including the hardy and popular indoor plant known as Kimberley queen. In the main gorge large pinky-mauve jellyfish, softly beautiful in their watery round shapes but nonetheless rather venomous-looking, floated past the dinghies. When we explored a mangrove-lined creek near the river's entrance, the water was so clear that it was easy to see the shoals of hurrying fish, and the huge three-metre-long shark that slid past the boat. Best of all were the two dugongs that surfaced briefly just in front of us, near the river's mouth; this caused such excitement among the photographers in our group that they fell over each other in a tangled heap as they rushed to the bow of the dinghy to capture these seldom-seen creatures on film. It was just as well the dugongs appeared several times!

The last river we explored before mooring at Wyndham was the Forrest, flowing into the extremely muddy Cambridge Gulf. At first it appeared a most dreary river, its character not

Cave paintings, Bigge Island

enhanced by the strong wind that whipped the water into very high waves; and it was as muddy as the Gulf. Erosion at the river's edge had undermined sections of the bank, exposing mangrove roots which dangled dismally in the air as they lost their grip on the soil. But once we entered sheltered side-creeks, where among the mangroves the atmosphere was distinctly secretive, it was more interesting. In one spot there was a colony of flying-foxes roosting high in the treetops. I tried to get a photo of them but it was impossible to find a good angle from the boat. 'Go up on the bank,' suggested Arie, the skipper. I looked at the exposed muddy bank and thought of the Malcolm Douglas films in which Douglas had sunk to his knees whenever he had to climb onto a bank along this coast; then I gazed longingly at the flying-foxes squabbling noisily amongst themselves. 'After you, Arie,' I replied, knowing he wanted a photo too. A brief look of dismay crossed his face, but after a moment's hesitation he climbed gingerly out of the boat and up to the bank. Fortunately, his feet sank only about 10 centimetres into the soft slimy mud, so I quickly followed. It was much better photographing the flying-foxes from under the trees.

Soon after leaving the Forrest River we moored at the great semicircular wharf at Wyndham. But our adventures were not yet over, because someone noticed four huge crocodiles sunning themselves on the banks just behind the town's main street. A dinghy was quickly launched, and we were able to get surprisingly close before they slipped into the water. The next morning another two large specimens hung around the *Kimberley Explorer,* looking very much as if they wanted a feed.

To think that we had to return to 'civilization' in order to see the biggest crocodiles of the entire trip!

Hunter River

Kings Cascades. In the small inlet at the cascades, vegetation clings to the rocky walls like hanging gardens, kept moist by a constant seepage of water that drips down the cliffs.

The *Kimberley Explorer*, moored in the Prince Regent River.

Camp Creek Falls, Prince Regent Reserve. The second tier of these falls drops into a large pool; only the pool above the falls is considered to be free from crocodiles and safe for swimming. Camp Creek is a tributary of the Prince Regent River, and the falls lie about eight kilometres upstream, of which the last three kilometres must be walked.

A dragonfly rests on the heart-shaped leaf of a white snowflake lily of the genus *Nymphoides*. This small, dainty waterlily carpets the still corners of creeks and backwaters in the Prince Regent Reserve.

At Tranquil Cove a few mangroves struggle to grow in a creek edged with craggy cliffs. This small but beautiful cove hides in the cliff-lined shore east of Cape Londonderry.

A pair of brown boobies guard their young chick and nest on the beach at the Lacepede Islands, west of Beagle Bay. Because the islands are a wildlife refuge, a permit is required to land there.

Facing page:

An aerial view of Prince Frederick Harbour, which lies off York Sound, about halfway between Derby and Wyndham. In the foreground is the mouth of the Hunter River.

Strangely weathered rocks—known as the 'Petrified Warriors'—line the shore at Llangi, a sacred Aboriginal site south of Kuri Bay.

The historic carving on this boab tree at Careening Bay was made by the crew of HMC *Mermaid* in 1820, when they spent some time here repairing their leaky cutter. Careening Bay lies off York Sound.

Two dugongs at the mouth of the King George River. They are considered to be rare throughout much of their traditional habitat in the Indian and West Pacific oceans, and it is believed that most of the world's dugongs inhabit Australia's northern waters. These herbivorous marine mammals can grow to three metres in length.

King George River. A boat is dwarfed by the towering 100-metre-high walls at one of the waterfalls—which ceases to flow during the dry season. Situated on the north coast about 150 kilometres from Wyndham, the gorge imprisoning the river runs for about 12 kilometres from its river-mouth to the twin falls.

A native hibiscus, Llangi.

Through drifting smoke from fires lit for the occasion, Aboriginal dancers at Kalumburu arrive to perform a corroboree.

Sunset at a beach near Kalumburu, in Deep Bay, off Napier Broome Bay.

Facing page:

One of the spectacular Kaiara or nautical Wandjina rock paintings that grace the wall of a cave on Bigge Island, in the Bonaparte Archipelago. Nobody knows who is responsible for these paintings, notably different from conventional Aboriginal art which depicts subjects mainly in outline form.

Cable Beach, Broome

*T*HE STARGAZERS

Somewhere,
out there,
in the light of the luminous galaxies,
or the dark of the fathomless cosmic seas
where drown the infinite mysteries
of Time and Space . . .

Somewhere,
out there,
I feel there is a face
whose eyes
at this very moment scan the skies
for evidence of Other Life —
a cosmic pulse,
a code, a rhyme? —
to signify the dream is shared
in Other Space
in Other Time.

Are we perhaps an Age too soon?
Perhaps an Age too late.
Together
though light-years apart,
we scan the skies
and wait . . .

NEROLI ROBERTS

The Ord River, downstream from the dam

TO THE EAST

SOME of northern Australia's loveliest scenery lies in the east Kimberley. Motoring through this region is a delight because, whether you are on the highway or exploring minor roads, just about every kilometre is packed with beauty. Craggy hills and ranges, many of them topped with high collars of bare rock, lie relatively close together, and if the road is not winding through hills, it runs over plains flanked by bold ranges that, although rising some distance from the road, are close enough to give the sense of being in a panorama. Above all there are the colours of the land: rich rusts, rose-pinks, soft purples, dark-chocolates, all heightened by the foliage, the flowering shrubs and the seas of brilliant-green canegrass that turn a warm gold once the wet season's rains have ceased. Throughout the day the countryside undergoes many wonderful colour-changes, depending on the direction of light.

Take a drive from Wyndham to Kununurra at sunrise, or from Lake Argyle to Kununurra late in the afternoon, and see how breathtaking the land is when the sun is low in the sky and causes the shadows to accentuate the folds in the hills; at these times the scenes are guaranteed to make photographers reach for their cameras and artists to scramble for their brushes. Even on the long run from Kununurra to Halls Creek it is impossible to suffer boredom, for the landscapes are constantly changing. Great ramparts of rock rear from the valleys and give way to rocky un-dulating terrain where some of the hills are covered with warm-coloured stones and boulders clustered so thickly that they might easily have been dumped there by a giant tip-truck. Near Bow River these bouldered hills are rather close to the road and present quite a spectacle.

The town of Kununurra is the gateway to the Kimberley for most travellers from the eastern states. Linked by 500 kilometres of bitumen to Katherine in the Northern Territory and situated by Lake Kununurra on the Ord River, Kununurra is the main town of the east Kimberley. The town was established in 1960 to serve the Ord River Irrigation Scheme. Completed in 1972, the Ord Dam traps the voluminous floodwaters of the Ord River, which is fed by cyclonic rains falling only between December and March. For centuries the Ord carried its abundance of life-giving water to the coast, where it was poured into the sea and wasted, leaving behind waterholes that would barely survive the dry season; but thanks to modern technology, plenty of water now flows in a network of channels that irrigate the district's crops. The crops did not flourish as everybody had planned, however. At first cotton was grown, but pests and diseases appeared on such a scale that it was not a viable proposition. Then they tried rice, but the flocks of birds, thriving because of the increased water in the region, moved in to feast on the crop. Today a variety of fruit, vegetables and fodder-crops are grown with some success but on a relatively small scale. One local summed up the situation: 'Kununurra is still waiting for a crop to be found that will put it on the map.' Meanwhile, everybody enjoys plenty of locally grown produce.

When I first visited Kununurra in 1975 the town was just beginning to shed its 'wild west' image. I heard about the station-owner who liked to land his helicopter in the main street in order to pick up his groceries; and about the bloke who angrily shot his neighbour's crowing cockerel one night because it kept him awake. On that first occasion the place reminded me of Canberra in its earlier years, when visitors always complained of either getting lost or driving around in circles. One of the locals told me that he had been at Kununurra for a year and was still getting lost. Signposts have now improved, though the last time I was in the town there was still no sign directing visitors to the shopping centre, which is placed well off the highway. But if you followed the signs to the Visitors Centre to enquire where the shopping centre was, you would automatically find it because the Visitors Centre is among the shops!

Today, Kununurra is a thriving township, about the size of Derby, and has the best shops and community facilities in the Kimberley; it even has a Celebrity Tree Park, where people of renown have planted trees. One blessing to the town has been the discovery of diamonds in the area. The Argyle Diamond Mine started operations in 1979 and is now the world's biggest producer of rough diamonds, accounting for a third of total world production. Workers commute daily by plane from Kununurra to the mine, situated about 100 kilometres by air to the south. It might sound a glamorous way to go to work, but one lass told me that she was airsick on nearly all the flights.

One of the most important economic contributions to the town is tourism. Kununurra may be waiting for a crop to put it on the agricultural map, but as far as tourists are concerned the town is firmly established as an excellent base from which to take in a multitude of attractions in an extremely scenic district. There is even a national park on its doorstep: Hidden Valley, situated one kilometre from the post office. This unique sandstone cul-de-sac is small, but what it lacks in size it makes up for in detail and character, as it is riddled with fascinating caves, crevasses and mini-gorges. Some of its features are reminiscent of the Bungle Bungle Range, to the south.

Every time I visit Kununurra I find something new to do; the last time it was one of the 'sunset' boat-tours that run on Lake Kununurra. Although friends with a boat had shown me the Ord River's everglade-like backwaters — where, since the making of the lake, a series of channels have formed through the vegetation to create a superb wetland area for wildlife — I had never been out on the lake at sunset. The best sunsets are seen when there is no wind to spoil the effect of the sun's colour spilling over the water, and no breeze to ruffle the reflections of the great razorback ridge known as the Sleeping Buddha, which turns a wonderful rose-pink at sunset. There was little wind the afternoon I took the tour, and the boat-trip was all it had promised to be — even the operator's commentary was as colourful as the scenery. We saw a lot of wildlife, including many freshwater crocodiles and a large black-headed water-python that surfaced near the boat.

However pressed for time you may be, there is one place to see which is a 'must': the Ord Dam at Lake Argyle, situated 67 kilometres from Kununurra. Many people think that some of the most impressive scenery to be found in the Kimberley's accessible areas is in the rugged Carr Boyd Range around Lake Argyle, and I am inclined to agree. The sheer grandeur of the range and the impact of colour around the Ord Dam are stunning; and every time I see the soft blue of the lake, set among the brightly coloured hills like a sapphire, infinitely precious, I feel as if I am part of a richly coloured oil-painting.

There are some good facilities at the dam. At Lake Argyle Village, located on a ridge close to the lake, a motel, camping-ground and shop make it possible for travellers to spend some time here. I always delight in making frequent visits to the numerous lookout points early and late in the day, when the ranges stand out in dramatic relief, gently moulded by their own shadows. The afternoon boat-cruise on the lake is always the best because the light is superb at that hour.

Another favourite spot at Lake Argyle is the picnic-ground by the river at the dam wall, where trees in the well-kept gardens provide good shade from the hot sun. For many years some very large freshwater crocodiles have lived on the opposite bank, and sometimes they are seen basking on the rocks. On most visits I have watched them through binoculars, intrigued by their prehistoric shapes and the trance-like stillness in which they lay sunbaking, often with their mouths wide open and displaying rows of teeth, as if smiling in lazy contentment. All crocodiles keep their mouths open from time to time when it is hot, because this helps to cool their bodies — just as dogs pant when they are hot. Despite their fierce appearance the freshwater crocodiles are very timid, but although considered to be harmless they have the equipment to inflict a serious injury if provoked. Many people are quite ready to swim in the Ord, but, along with some of the locals, I do not share that readiness. These waters may be home for freshwater crocodiles, but every now and then the dangerous saltwater species is sighted; indeed, some locals believe it is only a matter of time before a salty takes up residence in the lake near the town and has a close encounter with someone. If this happens, I suspect the croc will not be permitted to stay around for long: too many activities take place on the lake to allow a resident salty to upset things.

Carr Boyd Range

Halls Creek lies 358 kilometres south of Kununurra. An increasing number of visitors enter the Kimberley through this town after coming up via the Tanami Desert. Travelling by this route, motorists have easy access to the Wolf Creek meteorite crater, the second-largest in the world (the largest is in the United States). Situated 146 kilometres south of Halls Creek, this great crater, measuring 850 metres in diameter, has created much worldwide scientific interest and is regarded as the closest in appearance to the craters seen on the moon's surface. It is not known just when the fragment from a 'shooting star' escaped disintegration into dust on entering the earth's atmosphere and landed about half a kilometre from the stream that gave the crater its name. Because the road to it is often rough and not kind to campervans, I decided to see the crater from the air. The flight from Halls Creek took twenty minutes and the pilot gave us a good look, flying around the crater many times at different heights, including a low-level sweep that enabled us to see the detail of the little forest of trees grouped in its centre. The crater looked tremendous from the air, and I suspect it is visually more interesting from above than from the ground.

Halls Creek is no longer a place where visitors just fill up their vehicles with petrol and drive on. Apart from being the closest town to the meteorite crater and the Bungle Bungle Range, Halls Creek has a rich history of goldmining. At long last someone is introducing its interesting past to the public. 'The General is the man you should see in Halls Creek,' a local in faraway Broome had suggested, and so I did. Nicknamed after the great American general of the Second World War, Graeme Macarthur is known more widely as 'The General' than by his real name. As well as running tours into the Bungle Bungle Range, this local entrepreneur, who knows the district inside out, also operates an excellent day-trip to the goldfields of the rugged hill-country behind the town, where the slopes are littered with fascinating mining relics.

I went with him on his Ruby Queen goldfields tour, which included a visit to some ruins at the old town of Halls Creek (the town was moved to its present site in 1948). The 25 kilometres of gravel out to the old town were in good condition, but the track to the goldfields was totally unsuitable for any kind of conventional car. The General explained that gold was first discovered at the headwaters of the Ord River in 1882; three years later the mining of payable gold triggered the state's first goldrush. Although the mining peaked in 1887, the largest mine, the Ruby Queen, continued until the 1950s and was the last to close. In recent years mining has recommenced in the area, and the finding of other minerals besides gold looks promising for the district's future.

The old mining area is in the process of being declared a Historic Site. On the tour we scrambled up stony hills and peered into the Ruby Queen's shaft, and into others that dropped a good 30 metres vertically into the ground; a few of the shafts were topped by the remains of windlasses. The most spectacular relics were at the site of the Ruby Queen's stamping-batteries, where, beside the ruins of an old brick building, the great machines rose in rusted splendour, almost forgotten memorials to this period of Kimberley history.

The General made the place come alive as he described the old mining days. 'Just imagine,' he said, 'ten thousand men crawling over these hills to scratch in the rock-hard ground for a bit of colour. Think of the dust, the flies, the heat which in summer remained in the forties for days on end — and there was precious little shade.' I asked him if there had been much lawlessness among the miners. 'I'll show you the policemen's graves in the old cemetery,' was his answer. Apparently it had been a pretty wild place, a small hell on earth isolated from the rest of Australia by vast distances. As we gazed around the dry barren hills studded with old mines, we couldn't help wondering at the extent to which men will suffer to get rich.

The Ord River and its wetlands, near Kununurra

Elephant Rock. Part of the Sleeping Buddha, this distinctive rock rises over the Ord River. The Sleeping Buddha's proper name is Carlton Ridge, but nobody seems to use that name.

For a few months during the dry season, every evening shortly after sunset streams of flying-foxes pour into the sky over Lake Kununurra to wing their way silently to feeding-grounds around the countryside. Well before sunrise they will return to their colonies across the river to hang upside-down to sleep.

Facing page:

Sunset on Lake Kununurra. This lake is also known as the Diversion Dam, which was built before the Ord Dam.

Between Kununurra and Halls Creek.

Near Kununurra, on the road to
Wyndham and Halls Creek. This is a
typical east-Kimberley scene during
the dry season: a carpet of yellow
canegrass, graced by a few boabs and
evergreen trees, sweeps towards a
distant warm-coloured craggy range.

Maggies Creek, near Wyndham.
Lying close to a rest-area by the
Wyndham road, this waterhole on
Maggies Creek dries up a few months
after the rains stop at the end of the
wet season. Until then, it is an ideal
place for hot and weary travellers to
take a cooling dip, even when it is
quite shallow.

Rocky hill-country, near Halls Creek.

One of the Ruby Queen stamping-batteries, relics of the goldrush days at Halls Creek.

Facing page:

An aerial view of the Wolf Creek meteorite crater, situated 146 kilometres south of Halls Creek. Nobody knows when the meteorite landed, about half a kilometre from the stream that gave its name to the crater.

The shopping centre, Kununurra.

Turkey-bush or Kimberley heather (*Calythrix exstipulata*), which flowers in winter and is commonly seen along many roadsides.

Hidden Valley

Hidden Valley at night: the moon in a boab tree

*H*IDDEN VALLEY AT NIGHT

Come away, white man, come away!
Come away in the fading light.
Stop watching the flight
of nocturnal bird,
for surely you've heard
the Brown People say
it's madness to stay in Hidden Valley,
in Hidden Valley at night!

Abandon the cool
of the cave.
Hasten past lily-pool
boab and grave,
for the Brown People say
only a fool
would stay in the Valley at night . . .

Haven't you noticed how soon
the healthy, red face of the moon
blanches to sickly white
when it shines on the Valley at night?

In the Valley at night
the sensitive ear
will hear
the hint of a scream!
In the Valley the trembling finger will trace
patterns on rock,
patterns like lace,
where once there swirled the turbulent race
of primeval river and stream.

In the Valley
the wind whistles all night long,
rattles branches
and whistles a clap-stick song
that the Dead once sang so well —
it sighs
as it whispers a Dreamtime spell
called up from the depths of an ancient well
of wisdom, and long-lost ritual . . .

NEROLI ROBERTS

Ord Dam, Lake Argyle

59

'Beehive' outcrops, Bungle Bungle Range

THE BUNGLE BUNGLE RANGE

IT HAS been likened to a lost city, the ruins of an ancient civilization, a series of Buddhist temples, a collection of beehives. A Filipino who was shown an aerial photograph of the place wondered if he was looking at rice-terraces.

The Bungle Bungle Range is one of Australia's most extraordinary landscapes. Just as extraordinary is the fact that until 1983 only the Aborigines, a few pastoralists, and government officers knew it existed in the remote country lying between Kununurra and Halls Creek. Today it is one of the most important scenic attractions in the West, and there are those who predict that before long it will rate with Ayers Rock and the Great Barrier Reef as a major tourist destination in Australia. Described as a geological masterpiece, the range rises from the plains as a great triangular massif. It is cut by ravines and bound by high cliffs that in places rise to 400 metres and give way to a multitude of weathered orange-and-black banded domes said to be the most dramatic examples of their type on earth. Geologists believe the massif is a marine deposit formed some 350 million years ago in the Devonian era; over the centuries it was fashioned by tropical rains that heavily eroded the sandstone.

The land around the range was first opened for pastoral purposes in the 1880s. Fifty years later, droughts and overgrazing by cattle and feral donkeys had left much of the country stripped bare and badly eroded. By 1967 there was such concern over the amount of sediment being washed down the nearby Ord River towards the planned Lake Argyle that the government resumed the lease and commenced a program of erosion-control and revegetation that still continues today. Until the unique massif was 'discovered' by an aerial filmcrew working in the area, there were no access-roads and the only reference on maps was to the abandoned Bungle Bungle Outstation, not to any range. Soon after the world heard about the range, the inevitable four-wheel-drive track was pushed through to its edge. By 1987 it had been declared a national park.

'The Bungles', as the locals call the range, lie 300 kilometres by road from Kununurra and about half that distance from Halls Creek. Many people see it only from the air; indeed, that remarkable flight has become a 'must' on the tourist itinerary. Although most leave from Kununurra, an increasing number of people fly out from Halls Creek because it is cheaper — but they miss seeing the Argyle Diamond Mine and Lake Argyle, which lie on the aerial route from Kununurra. On one occasion I decided to charter a small plane that was licensed to fly with the passenger's door removed, because taking photographs through air is so much better than through perspex. At Halls Greek this was easily arranged: I had barely arrived at the caravan park when the pilots from Kingfisher Aviation made their daily round among the campers to book flights. I made mine for just after sunrise. It was a memorable flight, and I was thrilled to have a bird's view of the cliff-faces, the steep narrow gorges that sheltered a surprising amount of vegetation, and the colourful domes rising from the plain like a mass of crazily upturned flowerpots. With no door next to me it seemed that half the side of the plane was missing, but there was a heightened sense of being part of the scene and I decided it was quite the best way to fly, even if it was rather breezy!

An aerial flight taken over the Bungles really whets the appetite to see them at ground-level. The last 55 kilometres from the Great Northern Highway to the range take about four hours of hard, rough driving; it is strictly for four-wheel-drive vehicles, and people towing trailers need to take extra care because the undulating rocky terrain can cause towbars to snap. Forget the caravan: they are banned in the national park because the terrain is too rough.

My plans to go with a friend fell through, so the Kununurra-based Safari-Trek took me on one of their regular tours. We camped for two nights on the north-west side at Kurrajong, the more scenic of the two camping areas set on the plain beside the range. The lack of beehive-like domes in this part of the park came as a surprise to some of the passengers, who had expected to see nothing but domes; our driver explained that the range became more 'Bungleoid' in appearance further south. We erected our tents by an old spreading bauhinia tree in a cleared spot fenced with high canegrass. Nearby stood many eucalypts, massed in lovely pale-yellow blossoms. Unfortunately we were not the only ones to find the flowers attractive: that night a colony of flying-foxes moved in to feed on the trees' nectar. If they had fed quietly like most creatures we wouldn't have minded, but they noisily squawked and squabbled for hours, making sleeping difficult. Dingoes howled, and one mournful call was close enough to send tingles down our spines. The next morning a dingo wearing a shabby-looking ginger coat appeared briefly at the edge of the camp before slinking off into the grass. Both nights were very cold, which for June was normal, and we missed not being able to sit around a warm campfire. But fires are not permitted because there is not enough wood in the park.

Some wonderful visual treats are to be found in the Bungles' gorges, which are quite different from others in Australia. Echidna Chasm lies just north of Kurrajong. When we arrived it was too early for sunlight to fill the narrow ravine, but the walls at the entrance glowed a warm red, providing a perfect backdrop for the dark shapes of the many Livistona palms growing there. Dead fronds crackled loudly underfoot as we made our way through the gorge, which narrowed to a metre near its end. After walking for thirty minutes and scrambling over great blocks of fallen rock wedged in the chasm, we came to a wall that marked the end of the gorge.

It took nearly two hours to drive from Kurrajong to Piccaninny Creek, at the southern end of the range. The last few kilometres passed through scenery unlike anything I had ever seen: domed formations were everywhere, standing as rocky outcrops or appearing as part of the range — which in places displayed a million little hills piled high upon each other.

From the carpark it was a short walk to Piccaninny Creek, which runs for about six kilometres before entering Piccaninny Gorge. We explored only around the creek; for safety reasons, walkers planning to go right through the gorge must register the walk with the rangers because it is possible to get lost in the numerous side-gorges. One of these, Cathedral Gorge, lies close to the carpark. This short but beautiful gorge ends in a spacious cavern, where still pools of water and the reflected light of the warm-coloured walls give the place a fantastic atmosphere.

On the way back to our camp we stopped at the other camp, Belburn, and filled our watercans at the bore; Kurrajong's bore had yet to be established. We arrived at the bore's pump just as some men from the local water board were testing its water; they declared it to be very low in salinity, which was good news, for campers tend to appreciate a decent cup of tea. In fact, the water was much better than the supply we had brought from Kununurra.

On this particular visit to the Bungles only a few places were open to the public, and knowing that access to other areas was once permitted, I was disappointed. We were told they had been closed for 'scientific research', but we suspected other reasons. 'It is a very political park,' commented a local in Kununurra — meaning that various groups, including the federal government, would like control of it. Soon after the road went through to the range, Aborigines from the Warnum community at Turkey Creek set up a permanent camp at the far-north-west end of the park. It was explained to me that they were affiliated not traditional owners of Purnululu (the Aboriginal name for the Bungles). A number of tribes from other areas have claims to the range too, because in the past they all visited it, leaving behind rock paintings, engravings and burial-sites. It is to be hoped that a management plan fair both to Aborigines and to other Australians will be developed.

Approach to the range, from Kununurra

An aerial view showing one of many creeks that run from the range, which covers 450 square kilometres.

The flowers and fruit of the inland bloodwood (*Eucalyptus terminalis*), at the Kurrajong camping-ground.

Facing page:

Many beehive-like domes line Piccaninny Creek, at the southern end of the massif. These formations have been worn over the centuries by tropical rains that heavily eroded the sandstone—and continue to do so.

High cliffs edge the Bungle Bungle massif in many places, and are best seen from the air.

Aerial view over Piccaninny Gorge. Many narrow gorges run off this large one.

Echidna Chasm. In the early-morning light some Livistona palms are silhouetted against the high walls of the gorge. This species of *Livistona* is unique to the Bungle Bungle Range, and is yet to be named. Echidna Chasm lies on the north-west side of the range.

Facing page:

In Piccaninny Creek.

A close view of the domes' surface. This sandstone rockface is very fragile and therefore unsuitable for climbing.

In Cathedral Cave

A HAND IN OCHRE

Her tribe has vanished with daughters and sons,
    all her people lie under the sand.
Nothing to prove that she'd ever lived
    but the faint outline of a stencilled hand.

In earth-red ochre, or charcoal line,
    so many caves with the same mute sign.
I trace the shape with a pensive finger,
    why do I linger?

An ancient sadness chills this place
    — that's why I stop and pause.
Dark sister without name or face
    I place my hand on yours.

The long unmeasured years divide us,
    too late, too late for meeting;
but in this quiet forsaken cave
    hands touch
            — in Greeting . . .

NEROLI ROBERTS

Early morning in Windjana Gorge

THE LIMESTONE RANGES

IN a past era when part of the Kimberley was covered by tropical seas, a 'great barrier reef' formed in the warm waters offshore. It was created by organisms different from those present in the coral we know today, and over a period believed to be 350 million years this ancient Devonian limestone reef was subjected to a complex saga of sedimentation, uplift and erosion. Cut by rivers and weathered into pinnacles, towers, deep fissures and caves, the reef is now exposed in a series of long narrow ranges that wind over the country for 300 kilometres and rise to heights of 100 metres between Derby and the Fitzroy Crossing district. In its walls are many well-preserved fossils that show the animals and plants of the prehistoric sea.

Two of the Kimberley's best-known and most popular gorges lie in these limestone ranges: Geikie and Windjana. Of the two, Geikie Gorge has the easier access and consequently receives more visitors — including virtually all coaches touring the Kimberley. Lying in the Geikie Range 20 kilometres from the settlement of Fitzroy Crossing and part of a small national park, Geikie Gorge imprisons the Fitzroy River for eight extremely scenic kilometres. Between April and October the rangers run boat-tours on the river twice daily from the car park and picnic ground. The boat goes very close to the cliffs, where an astonishing variety of colourful markings, cavities and clefts riddle the walls. Solid bastions of chunky rock give way to areas agape with holes that resemble pieces of distorted empty honeycomb, and in numerous places the rock surfaces are pitted with a profusion of thumb-like indentations; in other spots it looks as if a bricklayer had been busy. Sometimes the cliffs overhang the water; elsewhere they are set well back from the banks, leaving space for lush green foliage to spread over the ground. The afternoon tour is the better one for seeing freshwater crocodiles sunning themselves on the rocky ledges and muddy banks; on both tours the birdlife is usually plentiful.

Swimming seems safe enough at Geikie, and a sandy area has been set aside for this activity a short distance from the camping-ground. On my first visit to the gorge I had asked the ranger about the dangerous freshwater sharks that were supposed to exist here, relics of the age when this area was part of the sea. He laughed and told me that back in the 1960s a story had gone around that a bloke had caught a grey nurse in the river, but nobody had seen the shark — or the bloke (maybe the shark had been caught over the bar of the local pub). There *are* small sharks here, as well as sawfish and some big stingrays; but these present no danger to swimmers because they live in the deep holes of the river — and the deepest one is about 90 metres.

There used to be a small camping-ground by the river at Geikie Gorge, but it has now been closed. This is just as well: who could forget the terrible bulldust raised by vehicles moving through the area? Even walking to and from the amenities block raised enough dust to keep you permanently grubby. At Fitzroy Crossing there are a motel and several camping-grounds. As the gorge is not far away it is easy enough to make a day visit and the road to it is now sealed.

Windjana Gorge lies in the Napier Range, 145 kilometres west of Fitzroy Crossing. Carved over the centuries by the floodwaters of the Lennard River and protected in a national park, this impressive gorge runs through the range for about five kilometres. By the time the tourists start arriving in the winter months the once-swollen river has ceased to flow, leaving only a string of pools that continue to shrink during the Dry. Motorists with caravans will find that access is easier from Derby than from Fitzroy Crossing, because the road between Leopold Downs and Fairfield stations is twisty and rough. Be careful about following advice from people who have not actually been on a road you intend to travel: at Fitzroy Crossing I met a couple in a sturdy four-wheel-drive vehicle that was not towing anything, and they had missed seeing Windjana Gorge because someone had told them he had heard that the road was too rough even for four-wheel-drives. On every trip to the Kimberley since 1975 I have been able to take my campervan along that track; it is all a matter of driving slowly — something many people find hard to do!

It may be a five-hour slow drive from Fitzroy Crossing to Windjana, but it is a very picturesque one. For much of the way grey limestone ranges provide a superb backdrop for tropical woodlands, grassy plains, many interesting boab trees, and a multitude of termite mounds. These mounds, a distinct feature of the tropical north, appear in all shapes and sizes and in colours that vary according to the soil. Most of the ones along this route are pale-brown or an earthy red, and are squat and knobbly creations looking very much as if they had been made from great handfuls of mud slapped together.

I love Windjana Gorge. Within the gorge's first kilometre before it turns sharply east, there is a wonderful sense of space which in no way lessens the sheer grandeur of the orange-splashed grey limestone walls that like a mighty fortress rise to 90 metres above the plain. Every time I visit Windjana some other lovely aspect is revealed. Particularly magical are the early mornings, when the gorge is partially flooded with a soft translucent light that barely lifts the veils of shadow clinging to the cliffs. If there is no wind the great walls are deeply mirrored in the long pools of water; and at this hour the reflections are dark and mysterious, waiting only for the sun to slip out from behind the massive rampart of rock to give them colour and life.

Clouds always give an extra dimension to scenes, and Windjana is no exception. One May morning when I was there I walked down to the pool by the large white rock and looked back towards the entrance. The sun had just risen over the wall and the gorge was flooded with warm sunlight and rich colour. Very quickly a mass of cottonwool clouds started to drift in from the west, and as they gradually filled the sky — and the pool with their reflections — the already beautiful scene took on a fantastic character that lasted until the clouds reached the sun and captured it.

Clouds may be great for artists and photographers, but in the Kimberley their presence often means warmer weather, which is not so great for camping. During this particular May visit the weather was unseasonably hot, and although I experienced some thrilling cloud-effects, day temperatures often peaked at 38°C with little relief at night. The van's fridge didn't like the hot weather either: when running on gas the lowest temperature it could manage inside was 22°C! (This is a common problem with certain types of campervan fridge: they work efficiently on gas only in cold weather.)

Despite the heat, there was good walking through the gorge because the path that ran between the river and the cliffs lay mostly in the shade. It was too hot for the freshwater crocodiles to be out sunbaking on the banks, though I did see what looked like straight knobbly logs floating on the surface of the pool. These crocodiles are now so used to people quietly walking past that they will not completely submerge when disturbed. After watching the 'logs' for a while and photographing a large cloud of noisy white corellas that festooned a nearby tree, I continued along the walking-path for a couple of kilometres. The vegetation was quite lush and tropical, and in spots the path went close to the water's edge. But any ideas of a nice cooling swim were quickly forgotten when I started to sink into the gluggy mudbank that effectively stopped access to the inviting water. It soon became apparent that I was the first person on the path that day, as numerous spiderwebs hung across it. Their owners were nowhere in sight, for which I was grateful because it was unpleasant enough just getting entangled in the sometimes hard-to-see webs; and judging by the size and strength of the strands, the spiders were probably big ones.

I may have missed the spiders but I wasn't so fortunate with another not-so-friendly inhabitant of the park. One night in the camping-ground I stepped out of the van to take some rubbish to a nearby bin and all but tripped over a huge mulga (king brown) snake. It was only a metre from the van's door, and lay like a straight rope as thick as a man's arm and about two metres long. Worse, it was in no hurry to move on. Seeing it in the light of the torch had stopped me from stepping on it — and (horror of horrors) I nearly hadn't bothered to take a torch! The lesson in this incident is that you should *never* be without a light when walking around bush-camps at night in northern Australia.

Another delight in the limestone ranges is Tunnel Creek, lying about one hour's drive east of Windjana Gorge. Here a 750-metre-long cave pierces the Oscar Range from one side to the other,

Termite mound, by the track to Windjana

and in the wet season a stream flows swiftly through the tunnel. During the winter months, when the water-level has dropped considerably, it is possible to walk right through, provided you don't mind wading in deep, cold water. The entrance to the tunnel alone is worth seeing. The huge cavern situated close to the carpark is almost blocked by a jumbled pile of boulders, many of them a musk-pink intricately laced with white. It is easy enough to scramble over the boulders and reach the dimly lit cave, where a deepening of the blackness ahead indicates the beginning of the tunnel walk.

If ever a walk required a companion or two, it is this one. I had attempted it alone some years ago. The atmosphere had been decidedly spooky and in the heavy blackness of the tunnel my strong torch was about as effective as a candle. I didn't get very far: after stumbling quite suddenly into a very cold pool of water that looked as dark and scary as its surroundings, I fled back to the entrance. Things weren't much better there either. I sat on a rock in the cave and wondered if

Geikie Gorge

anybody would arrive with whom I could do the walk. The silence in the cave was absolute — until a slow, slithering sound started up among the rocks horribly close to my feet. It wasn't long before the head of an olive python emerged. It stared at my frozen form in a coldly appraising manner, then moved into another rocky crevasse. But although the snake's head had disappeared, its body certainly hadn't, and I watched in fascination as the rest of it kept coming . . . and coming. Olive pythons can grow to three and a half metres in length, and I'm sure this one was every centimetre of it.

A few years later I was able to walk through the tunnel with three adventurous companions. We used fluorescent lanterns, which lit the ground immediately in front of us, and because it was late August there was not much water around — which was a relief, because a few months earlier we could have had water up to our chests. As we approached the halfway mark, natural light started to filter through from a shaft created by a collapse in the roof. I had heard about this collapse but was not prepared for its uncommon beauty: rocks and roof were reflected in the long pool, and tree-roots dangled like streamers, weirdly decorating the eerie cave. It took us twenty minutes to walk through the entire tunnel.

Boat-tour in Geikie Gorge

A storm about to break over the Napier Range, near Tunnel Creek.

A great bowerbird displays outside his bower, Windjana Gorge.

Facing page:

In Tunnel Creek. This is the rockfall section, about halfway along the cave's 750-metre-long tunnel, where part of the roof has collapsed.

A sand-goanna, Windjana Gorge.

The entrance to Tunnel Creek is almost blocked by a jumbled pile of boulders, many of them musk-pink intricately laced with white.

The Oscar Range, near Fitzroy
Crossing. This grey limestone range
was once part of the ancient coral
reef that formed in an earlier period,
when this area was a sea. The range
is one of a series that winds over the
plains for about 300 kilometres
between Fitzroy Crossing and Derby.

In Windjana Gorge, looking towards the entrance. The gorge's massive limestone walls tower over long pools left after the last annual flooding of the Lennard River. By the end of the dry season nearly all of these pools will have disappeared; the one shown here is permanent, and is home for a number of harmless Johnstone's freshwater crocodiles.

Geikie Gorge. The degree of beauty at any given time depends on the weather: if there is no wind at all, the coloured cliffs reflect superbly in the Fitzroy River.

Over the centuries the river has worn down Geikie's fossil cliffs to their present height of around 12 metres. The erosion still continues during each wet season, when the walls are washed by the floodwaters that race through the gorge.

Facing page:

A close view of Geikie's cliffs.

Johnstone's freshwater crocodile (*Crocodylus johnstoni*).

A small colony of sleeping flying-foxes.

81

Sunrise in Windjana Gorge

FABRIC PICTURES

On high
spiralling kites in feather stitch
enrich
a faded denim sky.
Below
a fold or two
of sturdy twill
artlessly creates a view
of hill
and dale
One linen sail
as pale
as milk
is appliquéd in threads of gold
on bright-blue-watered silk.

These are the pictures that I love
above
all others,
pictures of boabs, rivers and ranges,
sunlight and shadow
that constantly changes,
satin sunrise,
soft-velvet butterflies,
echidna quill
and brolga feather,
woven together
with skill
and love
by the Hand
that planned the Overall Pattern
from a vantage-point Above.

I think of this land
as a magic loom
and the shuttle as Passing Time,
and I've borrowed a few rich Kimberley threads
and woven them into rhyme.

NEROLI ROBERTS

At the Pentecost River crossing

THE GIBB RIVER ROAD

THE Gibb River Road is the shorter 'back road' that links Derby and Wyndham. Its 646 kilometres pass through a feast of glorious scenery that lies in some very wild and remote country north of the Great Northern Highway. Although it cuts off about 230 kilometres in distance for motorists who would otherwise have to travel via the longer route through Halls Creek, it is no time-saver because it is unsealed and in places extremely rough.

Construction started from the Derby end in the 1960s to enable cattle to be trucked from the Gibb River and Glenelg stations to the Derby abattoirs; this replaced the 'air beef' program in which the animals were slaughtered on the station and the meat flown out. Once the 'beef road' had reached Gibb River it was gradually pushed through to Wyndham. But the Main Roads Department was given responsibility for maintaining only the Derby-Gibb River section, leaving the remaining 280 kilometres to the East Kimberley Shire Council, which, unlike the Main Roads Department, simply does not have the money or resources to keep it in as good a condition as the Derby end. Tourists who grumble about it should spare a thought for the district's station folk, who regularly have to rattle their way over the road.

The Gibb River Road route is not recommended for conventional vehicles or caravans, but once the Wet's rains have ceased and the graders have been over the road, conventional cars can usually get through from Derby to Wyndham if extreme care is exercised — travellers should first check the road's condition with the shire authorities or the police. The worst section is invariably the 150 kilometres between Gibb River and Jack's Waterhole; it is also the least interesting. For those who don't want to risk shaking their vehicle to bits on this section, I recommend they explore the Gibb River Road in two 'bites': in the east travel from Kununurra as far as Jack's Waterhole, and in the west from Derby to Mount Barnett Station. I first drove the full length of the road in 1980, and my van had no trouble coping with the rocky sections, the corrugations, and the numerous large holes filled with thick bulldust. Some years later I planned to do the same trip, but a number of people who had been through advised against it because the Wyndham end was in a frightful condition — one man who had managed to get his Volkswagen 'Beetle' through described it as a nightmare. I decided not to put the van at risk and visited both ends separately. During the 1990s some work has been done on the eastern end; however, motorists still need to check its condition before attempting it.

Apart from the state of the road, the most commonly asked question concerns the availability of petrol along the way. It is sold at Mount Barnett Station, 310 kilometres from Derby, and at Jack's Waterhole, 218 kilometres further on. On one trip I had considerable difficulty finding out if unleaded petrol was available at Mount Barnett; everybody said it should be, but nobody was sure if the station actually had it. In the end I carried my own fuel, having been told that some tourists and a commercial tour had been unable to get service at Mount Barnett because the new owners of the station had not been there. As it turned out I need not have carried the petrol, but in this region it is essential to do so if there is any doubt about its availability. Soon afterwards a roadhouse was built by the road at Mount Barnett.

On this particular trip I had left Derby, well stocked with provisions, for Mount Barnett. Shortly after the Windjana Gorge turnoff the road entered the King Leopold Range. It took me more than a day to travel the 70 kilometres through this magnificent hill-country, which constantly changed in character and colour — it wasn't the road that made travel so slow, but the photography! As I passed the Lennard Gorge turnoff I wished somebody would make this spectacular gorge more accessible. Some years back I had explored the track and had found it barely fit for four-wheel-drive vehicles, let alone campervans. Apparently it is an extremely rugged gorge, and if you *did* manage to cover the six kilometres to it, either by vehicle or on foot, you would need to be a mountain-goat to climb down in to the gorge.

The King Leopold Range gave way to a series of mesa-like hills that extended to the Phillips Range, which sheltered the lovely Adcock and Galvans gorges. The eight kilometres into Adcock Gorge looked as if they hadn't seen a grader for years, and the wheel-ruts deeply gouged into the dry mud made driving difficult. From the carpark it was only a few minutes' walk to the first pool, which lay by a cliff, and after clambering up some rocks I came to the superb large main pool set at the base of high rock walls; this was an ideal place for a swim. Access is much better to Galvans Gorge, which is only one kilometre off the road. This gorge is small, but its pool and trickling waterfall give the place a charmed atmosphere.

My favourite gorge in this area is Manning Gorge, situated just beyond the camping-ground on Mount Barnett Station. Before my first visit a tour-operator had told me that when he took a group of tourists there they became 'drunk' with its beauty. Such stories can leave you with unrealistic expectations, but if this gorge is explored properly there will be no disappointment. As I photographed its imposing entrance at sunrise, memories returned of a day I had spent with friends walking through the gorge to the pool at the end. It had been a challenging walk, for in places we had to pick our way over gigantic boulders that littered the floor, and towards the end it had been necessary to scramble up the rough hillside and walk along the hot clifftop for a while before descending again. At the end of the gorge we almost collapsed into the deep (and surprisingly cold) pool to seek relief from the heat. Although on the way up I had enjoyed the beauty of the gorge, with its colourful craggy cliffs, lush vegetation and rockpools decorated with exquisite waterlilies, it wasn't until I made the return journey in the late-afternoon light that I caught something of the unique atmosphere of the place. The pleasant fanning breeze had dropped and everything was mirrored sharply in the many pools, giving the gorge a tremendous sense of depth and beauty.

There remained one more gorge to see: Barnett Gorge, about 25 kilometres further east. This was another favourite, for at sunset the splendid walls that line the pool turn a fiery orange, spilling vivid colour over the water. But I had to miss seeing it, as the track in from the main road was so dreadful that I couldn't get the van in. Needless to say I was more than a little frustrated, for in the past I had had no trouble driving to the carpark.

A couple of weeks later I was in Kununurra and set off for the eastern end of the Gibb River Road. From the moment I left the Wyndham road the country was interesting, and because the road's stony surface was conducive to slow driving, there was ample opportunity to drink in the beauty and detail of the passing scenery. The craggy rolling hills and massive rocky outcrops gave way to the dramatic Cockburn Range, a huge plateau-topped massif that wore fantastic collars of pinky-brown rock; at the foot of its western end lay the Pentecost River. Knowing that the river-crossing was only five kilometres upstream from its mouth at the crocodile-infested Cambridge Gulf, and that the muddy water below the crossing was an ideal home for crocs, I camped well away from the river. At sunset the brooding Cockburn Range became swathed in shades of pink and red that glowed warmly against the evening sky, providing a marvellous backdrop for the Pentecost River. There were several good photographic vantage-points on the hills on both sides of the river, but the prettiest views I was to see of this range were from Home Valley Station.

Before reaching Home Valley, situated a few kilometres from the crossing, I had to negotiate the crossing itself, which I rather dreaded. The last time I had taken a campervan across it, the stones had been so big and chunky that the extremely hard steering required to get the van over them had left my arms feeling as if they were about to drop off; apart from that, I was now in a van that had a lower ground-clearance. However, my concern was needless: although the stones were still there and it was necessary to drive very slowly, recent roadwork had smoothed the surface considerably. Except for a small pool in one spot, there was no water on the crossing. The Pentecost is tidal here, but once the floodwaters have receded after the Wet, the river covers the crossing only at very high tides.

At Home Valley Station visitors are welcome and lodge-style accommodation is provided. I had heard that there was some wonderful scenery on the station, and that the owners, the Sinnamon family, ran tours into this country. The Sinnamons came to the Kimberley in 1978 from cattle properties in Queensland, and amalgamated Home Valley, Durack River and Karunjie stations; eight years later they opened Home Valley for visitors, providing scenic and fishing tours of the

Barnett Gorge

district. By 1988 a lodge had been built at Jack's Waterhole, a permanent pool on the Durack River. I spent a couple of days at Home Valley and, like most who stop there, discovered the hospitality so warm that I might have been visiting friends, not staying at a commercial lodge.

Before we visited Oomaloo Falls, Cameron Sinnamon took our small group to Jack's Waterhole, which is located close to the Gibb River Road and an hour's drive from Home Valley. For many years this has been a popular campsite for travellers passing through, offering good shade and a safe place for swimming. It was with mixed feelings that I viewed the changes that had taken place at the waterhole since my last visit. Even the name had changed! I had known it as 'Joe's Waterhole', but Ian Sinnamon was quick to point out that it had originally been named after Jack Campbell, Karunjie's head stockman up to the 1950s, and that when the Main Roads Department pushed the road through to Wyndham the waterhole was renamed after Joe, one of the workmen. This upset the locals and for years they tried to get the name changed back; so the Sinnamons corrected it when they developed the waterhole. Some people are not happy that the place has been developed, but the Sinnamons had no choice: the area had become a veritable dustbowl from overuse, and many of the campers never bothered to take out their rubbish. The waterhole now looks clean, with grass growing where dust once lay; and the hot showers are a welcome luxury in this dusty, remote area.

On the way to the Oomaloo Falls we passed through some very picturesque country: many odd-shaped boab trees clung to the rocky, rust-coloured slopes that rose above seas of high canegrass; there were kurrajongs in flower, their red blooms standing out amongst the trees' leafless branches, while splashes of vivid yellow from the showy elephant-ear wattle enhanced the already colourful scene. We sighted quite a few donkeys. These feral animals do more damage to the environment than cattle because their hoofs are sharper and they graze closer to the ground. A widespread eradication program has been mounted in the Kimberley. The extent of the donkeys' numbers was shown when, in an area of around 400 square kilometres, more than 4500 of the animals were shot in six days. There are plenty of feral cats too, and it is not uncommon to find specimens weighing 12 kilograms — which is a lot of cat. Many tourists are now aware of the environmental problem posed by feral cats; and it is unlikely that I will ever again experience the extraordinary scene I once witnessed at Windjana Gorge, when campers put out saucers of milk for the feral hordes that roamed the park, regarding these efficient destroyers of wildlife as 'poor lost pussies'. (This was before the mobile rangers were based there.)

From the top of the range Oomaloo Falls presented an impressive spectacle, even though no water flowed over the sheer semicircular rock wall that dropped 60 metres to a large pool fringed with thick vegetation. After walking around the extensive rim of the falls, we drove on to the Durack River and spent the afternoon exploring and swimming in a beautiful pool downstream from the Durack Falls. At another spot by the river Cameron showed us some cave paintings in a small rocky overhang, but the paintings had not been touched up for many years and the elements had taken toll of some of the designs. However, meeting the overhang's inhabitants made up for any disappointment with the paintings: we found six splendid tree-frogs huddled together in a dark corner. These large frogs with yellow spots on their bright-green bodies were most attractive, and naturally I was very keen to photograph them. After a pantomime consisting of a number of very indignant frogs jumping in all directions with humans trying frantically to catch them, I asked Cameron to calm the two captured ones by placing his hands gently over their bodies while sitting them on the rock; for a few seconds they posed quietly for some quick photographs.

We returned to Home Valley tired, but ready for one of the homestead's delightful baronial-style dinners by candlelight.

Cockburn Range

Manning Gorge at sunrise. This is the entrance to the main part of the gorge, situated on Mount Barnett Station, about 310 kilometres from Derby. There are two good walks from the camping-ground: the first is over the hills to the large pool and waterfall at the end of the gorge, and the second through the gorge itself to the pool and falls.

Galvans Gorge. This small but very beautiful gorge lies in the Phillips Range. Access is easy, as the gorge is only a kilometre off the road, about 285 kilometres from Derby. From the carpark it is a good five minutes' walk to the spacious pool and waterfall, which during the dry season is only a trickle.

The top pool at Adcock Gorge, in the Phillips Range.

Stockmen take cattle across the road, near the Drysdale River turnoff.

Facing page:

Bold Bluff at sunset. This view is from the road near Bell Creek, just north-east of the King Leopold Range.

Elephant-ear wattle (*Acacia dunnii*). This plant is named for its leaves, which resemble elephants' ears in shape.

Kurrajong flower (*Sterculia viscidula*).

Mount Hart, in the King Leopold
Range. Rising to 661 metres and
bound by great slabs of rock, it is one
of the most distinctive landmarks in
the range visible to travellers on the
Gibb River Road. The King Leopold
Range is a worn and dissected
escarpment at the edge of the
Kimberley plateau, and stretches
for about 225 kilometres.

Durack River. Clouds reflect in a
long pool downstream from the
Durack Falls, late in the afternoon.
This pool is one of several large
permanent waterholes that remain
throughout the dry season; once the
rains come in the Wet, the river
flows swiftly and empties into
Cambridge Gulf.

Precipice Range, between the King Leopold Range and the Phillips Range.

Jack's Waterhole. Lying close to the road, this waterhole is a popular resting-place for travellers.

Facing page:

Oomaloo Falls. They are situated on private property, and the only way to see them is by joining a tour from Jack's Waterhole.

Giant waterlilies (*Nymphaea gigantea*) are seen in many quiet pools throughout the Kimberley.

A boab at moonrise

THE SOLITARY TREE

A solitary tree
floats in a whispering sea of grass.
A shoal of pelicans drift by
along the ocean of the sky.

The tree by day
is a castaway,
by night
a coral form bleached white
by timeless tides of lunar light.

But night or day
in some strange way
it stands enshrined
becalmed and tranquil
in an isolated bay
of my mind...

NEROLI ROBERTS

Mitchell Falls, western side

THE MITCHELL PLATEAU

I HAD never heard of the Mitchell Plateau until I first travelled the Gibb River Road and met some people at Jack's Waterhole who had just been there. They strongly recommended it, and spoke enthusiastically about a place called Surveyors Pool. I asked if the area was suitable for campervans. 'No way!' one of them replied. 'The roads are very rough and there are some pretty steep jump-ups.' ('Jump-up' is a term commonly used in the north to describe a road that goes up a hill of any height, from three to 300 metres.) I had to wait many years to see the plateau because until recently no local tours to the area were available from the Kimberley towns; in fact, few travellers ventured there at all. Today, tours operate out of Derby and Kununurra, and more and more people are going there.

Lying inland from Admiralty Gulf on the Kimberley's north coast, the Mitchell Plateau is situated about 230 kilometres north-west of the Kalumburu turnoff from the Gibb River Road. The first European to cross the plateau was William Easton, when he led a state-government expedition to the north Kimberley in 1921. In 1965 an extensive bauxite deposit was discovered on the plateau. By the mid-1980s many people believed that a national park was more needed here than a bauxite mine, and the Australian Conservation Foundation called for the plateau to be placed on the World Heritage List.

I joined Safari-Trek's first tour of the season to the Mitchell Plateau. Starting from Kununurra, we flew to Kalumburu, where our tour leader-driver met us in a four-wheel-drive vehicle to take us to the plateau, with a planned return to Kununurra via the eastern end of the Gibb River Road. Our small group left Kununurra on a warm afternoon in May for the one-hour flight to Kalumburu. After spending two nights at a pleasant beach-camp on the shore of Napier Broome Bay and seeing something of the area, we headed for the plateau's turnoff, about 110 kilometres south of Kalumburu.

Shortly before reaching the plateau we crossed the scenic King Edward River. Fortunately it was lunchtime when we arrived and there was time to look around; indeed, it was a place where you could happily spend days exploring the riverbanks or dallying around the edges of the water. Downstream, and just before the waterfall tumbled into a large and deep pool, an expanse of polished red rock covered the flat ground beside the river. Its gleaming surface was dotted with an amazing variety of holes, some very large, others quite tiny, that were so round and smooth that they looked as if they had been fashioned by a stonemason.

We finally reached the Mitchell Plateau after the vehicle had climbed a long, steep hill. Once we were there the vegetation changed noticeably, and it wasn't long before we were driving through a forest of Livistona palms that covered large tracts of the area. Nowhere in Australia had I seen anything like this, and at first I couldn't believe my eyes — I had heard there were palms on the Mitchell Plateau, but not *forests* of them. Eucalypts intermingled with the palms and sometimes took over completely, but mostly the Livistonas were the dominant vegetation. Apparently there used to be many more of these palms, in places so thick that they resembled dense green walls along the road, but in recent times forest fires have thinned their numbers.

So far, mining activities have been only at the exploratory level, and although one company still holds the lease, there are no immediate plans to start removing the extensive but low-grade bauxite deposits. This is just as well for the plateau: when operations start, the mining company plans to scoop the ground's surface in order to remove the bauxite — which in the process will strip the vegetation and soil-layers bare. Promises have been made to replant, and this could probably be done successfully enough with the eucalypts; but not with the ancient Livistona palms, which took centuries to grow. According to one person I met, the mining company's record so far has not been good on the plateau. 'They've done enough damage already. Some pretty big holes have been left that should have been filled in,' the man said, then added that it was doubtful the plateau would ever be mined. 'The greenies won't let them.'

The palms are not the plateau's only unique feature: 39 species of mammals have been recorded — which is the largest number noted from any area of comparable size in Western Australia — as well as 86 species of reptiles and amphibians, including a newly discovered frog. There is some excellent scenery too, and many people are now coming here just to see one outstanding sight: the Mitchell Falls.

The Mitchell Falls lie on the Mitchell River, about 20 kilometres from the now abandoned caretaker's camp by Camp Creek; the last three kilometres have to be walked. We left our base camp at Camp Creek early in the morning for an excursion to the falls. At the carpark a sign advised that six hours must be allowed for the return journey, which struck me as a rather long time for a three-kilometre walk. At the end of the day, however, I had to agree with the sign: all six of the hours had been required. The heat and the very rugged terrain considerably reduced our walking speed, and in many places time was lost hunting for the yellow discs that marked the route. They were often hard to find, and set either high in trees or low on boulders; or they metamorphosed into piles of stones or oddly placed sticks to indicate the way. Once we were at the falls — and had taken a much-needed and refreshing swim — plenty of time was required to see them properly.

A short distance before the falls, the scrubby vegetation through which we had been battling along Mertens Creek suddenly opened out to an expanse of rock into which was cut the narrow but incredibly deep Big Mertens Gorge. The creek spread into a pool at the top of the gorge, just short of spilling over the perpendicular side to the water that lay far below. After wading through the shallow top pool, followed by a five-minute scramble over the rocky hill, we came out to the head of the Mitchell Falls. The sight of about a dozen people wandering around seemed oddly out of place after our wilderness walk, but there had after all been four camps at the carpark.

At the head of the falls, all we could see was the river disappearing into a great gorge; so to view the falls it was necessary to walk along the clifftops that flanked the river. None of us had any idea what to expect — even our driver was here for the first time. I had seen no photographs of this place, nor talked to anyone who had been here, and I expected to see just another attractive waterfall tumbling into a pool. I certainly wasn't prepared for the remarkable picture that opened up as I clambered over the chunky rocks that topped the cliffs. Four main falls cascaded over the rust-coloured, craggy rims of the tiered gorge; one of the tiers displayed three separate white curtains of water which gave a tremendous dimension to the scene. Only two tiers were visible from the eastern side, at which we had arrived, but when we crossed the river — a hazardous task to say the least for anyone carrying camera equipment, as the rocky bottom was very slippery — the scene revealed all four tiers and even grander views of the falls. Considering how poor the recent wet season had been, there was quite a lot of water pouring over the tiers, and although it was impressive I knew that during the Wet the falls would be a really fantastic sight. We were fortunate to see water at all: three weeks later I met some people who had just been there and they reported that the falls had dried up.

Surveyors Pool lay 44 kilometres north of Camp Creek, of which the last four kilometres had to be walked. I was looking forward to seeing this place, but there was some doubt as to whether we would get there. Rod, our driver, had been told that the track to the carpark was too rough for vehicular access, and that the rest of the route was poorly marked and so overgrown with high canegrass that it would be impossible to find the way. We even heard from some fellow-travellers that a team representing a prestigious Australian magazine had given the pool a miss after being warned they would be risking their lives! On the positive side, we knew of one couple who had gone there the previous week and *had* lived to tell the tale. Rod very sensibly decided to make at least an attempt to find the pool.

Again we left base camp early in the morning. The track to the carpark was badly washed away in places, but we took it very slowly and the vehicle got through. Wheeltracks continued down the hill from the carpark, but the washaways here were a miniature version of the Grand Canyon, with yawning chasms up to four metres deep. It was only a five-minute walk to the bottom of the hill — and the first orange marker. The markers were inadequate so we added yellow ones of our

King Edward River

own, but it soon became obvious that all we had to do was follow the old wheeltracks that ran over the plain. After nearly an hour of easy walking, the short grass gave way to woodland and high canegrass; the wheeltracks suddenly disappeared, and so did the orange markers.

Rod climbed a tree to take a better look at the country but hastily retreated when an army of biting green ants descended on him. The vegetation showed that there could be a stream in the vicinity so we pushed through the grass and trees, leaving plenty of our yellow markers behind. It wasn't long before we came upon the creek that had left the woodland, and after we had walked for about ten minutes up a most uninteresting creekbed, surrounded by an equally dreary plain, the ground suddenly opened up to reveal one of the most beautiful pools I have seen in the outback. In astonishment we gazed down on a deep spacious pool guarded by six-metre-high walls of craggy white King Leopold sandstone leached with grey, rust and pink markings. It was breathtaking. Access to a rocky ledge by the water was easy enough where the stream trickled down some step-like rocks to the pool. Except in one spot at the far end opposite the waterfall, the pool was surrounded by sheer walls. After a swim and some lunch we very reluctantly walked back to the vehicle. On the whole, it had been a far easier excursion than the one to the Mitchell Falls.

Before returning to the camp, we continued on the Port Warrender road to a lookout point which gave superb views over Admiralty Gulf. A notice warned that crocodiles and sandflies abounded at the port, and that the road to it was badly washed out. It didn't sound a very inviting place. Apparently the extensive mudflats are treacherously soft when exposed at low tide, so that anyone attempting to hunt for the bountiful mudcrabs living there is liable to sink in the mud; and it is dangerous to camp too close to the beach because of the crocodiles. Port Warrender had been chosen as a staging-point to bring in supplies to the mining camp — and to ship out the bauxite once mining started. We tried to drive in, but the last four kilometres were impassable.

Most people visiting the plateau like to camp at the Mitchell Falls carpark. We preferred the abandoned caretaker's camp because there was much more shade that effectively kept our tents and foodstores cool all day. However, we could have done without the wild scrub-bull that visited our camp each night. It was bad enough hearing him bellow as he crashed noisily through the scrub around the camp, but when he started to munch grass only a metre from where my head lay at the open end of the tent, I wasn't at all happy. Unlike the others' solid canvas tents, mine was a little nylon one that I had brought with me, and I had a nightmarish vision of the bull charging the tent in fright if he tripped over the guy-ropes well-hidden in the grass. Lone scrub-bulls can be extremely dangerous animals. Many years ago one pastoralist warned me to be very careful of these 'mean beasts that have personalities like twisted sandshoes' and can escape the annual musters for anything up to twenty years. Although the Mitchell Plateau has never been leased for grazing, wild cattle from adjoining leases wander up here from time to time.

In the morning the bull was still around the camp; I thought he looked rather lonely. After breaking camp we left the Mitchell Plateau for the Drysdale River. The following day we were on the Gibb River Road and spent our last night of the trip at Jack's Waterhole.

Surveyors Pool

Mitchell Falls, from the eastern side of the Mitchell River. They lie about 20 kilometres from the abandoned mining caretaker's camp.

Livistona palms (*Livistona eastonii*). Unique to the plateau, this species of palms is the most striking feature of the vegetation. Along valleys and creeks the vegetation changes to a more open woodland of eucalypts and other trees, including pandanus palms.

Facing page:

Big Mertens Gorge. Mertens Creek enters the Mitchell River near its falls, a short distance downstream from this gorge. The three-kilometre walk over rough terrain to the Mitchell Falls follows Mertens Creek for parts of the way.

Camp Creek, at the crossing by the abandoned caretaker's camp. An extensive low-grade bauxite deposit was discovered on the Mitchell Plateau in 1965, but only exploratory work has been carried out.

Mulla mullas (a species of the genus *Ptilotus*) carpet an open stretch of ground near the airstrip by the abandoned caretaker's camp.

Facing page:

Surveyors Pool, from a ledge at the water's edge. Situated on Currbirri Creek, this large isolated pool is surrounded by six-metre-high walls of King Leopold sandstone.

Brolgas in a small creekbed.

An overhang containing rock paintings, Mitchell Plateau

Cave paintings, Mitchell Plateau

CAVE PAINTING

The track to the cave
was made by the feet
of men who were brave and black.
The track from the cave was made by a tribe,
the tribe that never came back.

So he waits in the shadows,
for shadows are kind
to his age, and his wasp-fouled hair.
But sometimes the shadows
are cruel and dark
as his fears, and his growing despair.

That other idols have taken his place
is something he's never learned.
He was placed on the wall,
— so he waits on the wall
for the tribe that never returned.

And he dreams of the time
when his lofty cave
was used as a sacred place,
where the lubras danced the Brolga Dance
with formal, stately grace.

He dreams,
while the spiders weave a shroud
over his fading face . . .

NEROLI ROBERTS

Boabs in early-morning light

BOAB MAGIC

A BOOK on the Kimberley would not be complete without giving space to the boabs, those extraordinary fat-trunked, swollen-limbed trees that are a symbol of the region and provide considerable entertainment for travellers.

No two trees are the same: each has its own individual character. They come in many intriguing shapes, some bordering on elegance, others resembling warty old goblins, grotesque yet full of charm; some are jaunty, while others look distinctly arthritic and rather grumpy. There are the lovers that endearingly entwine their limbs around each other, and the mothers, whose plump maternal boles are surrounded by clusters of slim young ones. There are 'double bungers' and 'triple bungers' — trees with split trunks that have continued to grow separately into curious shapes — and grandfather-boabs that have managed to retain single trunks along with splendid arrays of gouty-looking limbs, and squat on the plains like obese characters from tales of fantasy. It's hardly surprising that one of the early explorers at first thought these trees were deformed by disease!

Growing on sandy plains, and stony hills so rocky that you wonder how it manages to hold root, the boab is confined to the north-west corner of Australia. Its botanical name is *Adansonia gregorii* and it is one of only two species, the other being found in tropical Africa. The tree's official common name on both continents is 'baobab', but Australians find this rather a mouthful and have shortened it to 'boab'. A commonly heard name is 'bottle-tree', but the boab is not to be confused with the true bottle-trees of Queensland which belong to the genus *Brachychiton*.

While their trunks are relatively slender, young boabs carry a certain grace which is enhanced in the light of a low sun because it causes their smooth grey bark to gleam like polished metal; but in age they develop distorted trunks and limbs, and their bark resembles the skin of an elephant. Some of these old boabs have trunks that expand to monstrous size, and display girths out of all proportion to their heights: a few have been known to attain a circumference of 24 metres, and a height of 20 metres. Understandably, horticultural books tend not to recommend them for the home garden — but this hasn't stopped Kimberley residents from growing them.

Boab trees fare well in drought conditions because the soft, fibrous wood of the trunk stores huge quantities of water from the wet seasons. The large fruit has a velvet-like outer covering; inside are the seeds and a dry pulp, which has an astringent taste and is said to be refreshing in humid weather. The Aborigines like to decorate the dried nuts: the outer skin is removed, and with a sharp knife they carve exquisite designs featuring birds, animals and human faces. Carved boab nuts have become prized among collectors of Aboriginal artefacts.

At the beginning of the Wet, when the fresh young leaves are about to appear, the boabs burst into bloom and this sight is guaranteed to warm the heart of anyone who loves flowers. The boab's bloom is magnificent. Exuding a delectably sweet fragrance that can be detected from the base of the tree when there are many blooms fully open, the large creamy petals unfold to reveal a spray of long stamens, the overall effect being one of essential femininity. As these deciduous trees gradually become covered in their green summer leaves, they lose much of their individual character, and instead of dominating the landscape they now quietly blend into the many greens of the wet season.

Soon after the Wet finishes, around April and early May, the leaves turn yellow before they fall. I found that the trees between Halls Creek and Kununurra displayed the showiest autumn colours, and I wondered if this was because they were further inland where the nights were cooler; many of the ones closer to the coast seemed to drop their leaves very quickly without showing much colour. By the time most visitors reach the Kimberley in June the boabs have lost their leaves, revealing a collection of naked, untidy limbs that resemble roots more than branches; it is at this time that they have such appeal. Boabs are wonderful subjects for the camera, and just beg to be photographed at sunrise or sunset when their fat trunks and the tracery of their limbs are silhouetted against the sky.

The *Adansonia* is capable of reaching many centuries in age: some stands in Africa are thought to be more than 5000 years old. In the east Kimberley, one tour-operator claims that some of the Kununurra boabs are around 1000 years in age, and that a 2500-year-old specimen is growing just over the border in the Northern Territory. I checked with the Botanic Garden in Perth and was told that there is little information on the longevity of Australian boabs. However, the director

A boab's branch growing towards the ground

pointed out that they do grow very slowly, giving as a good example the Careening Bay boab which features the historic carving HMC MERMAID 1820: since the letters show little distortion by subsequent growth, the tree must have been virtually the same size in 1820. If the tour-operator was right about the age of some of Kununurra's trees, the contorted, ancient-looking boab shown on this page could be *very* old indeed.

One boab with a 14-metre girth that looks very old is the Prison Tree at Derby. The Kimberley's most renowned boab, this hollow tree is reputed to have once been used as a temporary prison for a group of offenders. Some people say this story is nonsense, while others claim it was a common practice to use old hollow boabs as overnight cells for prisoners being escorted to the nearest town (there is another 'prison tree' near Wyndham which seems to have firmer historical evidence to support its claim). Lying on the outskirts of the town near the old cattle-yards, the Derby Prison Tree is a much-photographed tourist attraction, and despite its heavy covering of graffiti — and its dubious history — this boab is certainly worth seeing.

A sprawling, very old boab

A boab at sunrise. Although
shortened to 'boab', the tree's official
name in both Australia and Africa is
'baobab'; in Africa it has collected
some colourful names, such as dead-
rat tree, Judas bag, sour-gourd,
calabash, and monkey bread tree.

Facing page:

Flower of the boab.

Boabs in autumn colours, near Halls
Creek.

The Prison Tree, Derby.

A carved boab nut.

Boabs at sunset

THE BOAB

A boab tree
once said to me,
'Look, I am so much bigger than you,
how does this make you feel?
Do you see me as virile, strong, self-reliant?
A tower of strength?
A gentle giant?

'My forest is so much greater than you,
how does that make you feel?
A fumbling, sightless
mole in a hole
— or a clear-eyed creature,
proud and tall,
part of the Infinite Whole?'

NEROLI ROBERTS

Boab in leaf, near Kununurra

*I*N THE WET

WHEN I first started photographing the Kimberley, the locals repeatedly told me, 'You should come back in the Wet, when everything is green.' So one February I did, and it turned out to be one of the most fascinating of all my trips to the area. Like many southerners, I had reasoned that if one did come to the Kimberley in the wet season, there wouldn't be much to see because of the rain and bad roads. Certainly access by vehicle is limited throughout the region — if the Wet is a heavy one the main highway is cut by floods in a number of places, sometimes for weeks — but in the east Kimberley it *is* possible to see quite a lot. And when it does stop raining and the sun shines, which is quite often, the landscapes are even more impressive than in the dry season.

I went by plane to Kununurra. Just before arrival it had stopped raining, and as I stepped out of the aircraft's door the extremely humid air hit me like a warm cloth. But it was not unpleasant; in fact, it was rather relaxing. Everybody enthused over the rain. Although it was already mid-February the Wet had only just started properly about a week ago, and the community had barely recovered from a particularly gruelling pre-Wet 'troppo' season. For me, the timing was perfect: over the next few weeks I would witness the vegetation's astonishing growth that takes place at this time of year.

I hired a vehicle in Kununurra, drove out to the Ord Dam and stayed at the Lake Argyle Village motel. The road was all bitumen, and although there was water running at a few of the creek-crossings, there was no problem getting through; only after prolonged rain do some of them rise to a level that makes the road impassable for a few hours. I marvelled at the scenery; somehow the country seemed to have come *alive*. The characteristic features of the dry season — warm browns and yellows, and blue empty skies — had vanished. Instead, under a heavy canopy of clouds, two vibrant colours dominated: the moist-looking earthy rust-red of the craggy ranges, and the lush greens of the vegetation, dominated by the almost too vivid English green of the young canegrass that carpeted the ground. And the boabs, no longer dry naked figures of fun, stood proudly on the green plains, respectably dressed in their leafy summer attire.

The next few days continued to be overcast but pleasant, for the dense clouds that effectively screened the sun's burning rays, and a cooling north-westerly breeze, prevented the humidity from becoming suffocating. Some rain fell, but only for short periods. I spent a good deal of time wandering around the lake's lookouts and along the banks of the Ord River. The large freshwater crocodiles down near the dam wall now appeared on the rocks only when the sun was well hidden behind clouds. A nursery of young ones, the smallest no more than 30 centimetres in length, inhabited a pond beside the road. They were extremely timid, and if anyone approached they almost tumbled over each other in their haste to reach what they considered to be the safety of the shallow water. When they are small they like to keep away from the large crocodiles, which, like the saltwater species, are not averse to eating their young.

One evening a lad from the village appeared at my door clutching a baby croc — he thought I might appreciate a closer look. It was about 12 centimetres long and looked remarkably like a cute toy, though the boy assured me that even this little fellow could easily deliver a nasty bite if provoked. Shortly afterwards Martha Murphy, the manager's wife, collected me for an excursion to look for much bigger crocodiles by spotlight in the river, near the dam wall. The night air was very warm and humid. Thunder rumbled belligerently in the distance, and lightning flashed incessantly, searing the black sky. The beam of our lights swept over the water, picking up what looked like bits of burning coal floating on the surface. These were the freshwater crocodiles' eyes, which glow a fiery yellow-orange (salties' eyes glow red). We counted ten crocs before returning to the safety of the village. There had been another intriguing sight at the river: fireflies were everywhere, their lights gleaming eerily in the beams of our torches. The first one I spotted was so bright it could have been the light of a passing aircraft.

The wildlife was much more plentiful than it had been in the Dry. There were many types of birds around. Red-backed robins flitted through the trees splashing bright colour against the green

Carr Boyd Range

vegetation and grey sky; I watched silver-crowned friarbirds feed on the nectar of large yellow blooms flowering in the motel's garden; and then there were stately jabirus, bustards, white-throated honeyeaters and a variety of finches — to name just a few that had been easy to observe. Not so easily seen but often heard was the rainbird (also known as the Indian koel), whose monotonous 'cooee' rang through the air at dawn, at dusk, and sometimes at night.

I sighted many euros and wallabies. For some time Albert Peterson, the powerhouse attendant at the dam, had been feeding two short-eared rock-wallabies early in the mornings. If the wallabies were not already waiting, like children eager for a treat, they warily made an appearance when Albert called. One morning a third wallaby watched from a distance, as if trying to make up its mind whether to risk joining the others. But thinking better of it, the marsupial slipped behind a rock, no doubt continuing to gaze longingly at the distant feast of white bread. Generally, when other wallabies attempted to share the food they were chased away by the regulars, who seemed to think they had territorial rights over the bread. In any case, these treats were shortlived: on my next visit to the Kimberley, Albert explained that he had stopped feeding the wallabies because the bread was getting too expensive (which was probably just as well, as white bread is not a good diet for any animal).

Stormclouds over Lake Argyle

Although I saw water-monitors and sand-goannas foraging around the banks of the Ord, I met no snakes — despite having been warned to watch out for the death-adders that were starting to appear. When I expressed disappointment to one of the workmen at the village, he offered to take me out to find some. On that expedition we hunted high and low, turning over rocks, peering into likely bushes and trees, but could not find any. Even in the toilets down by the dam wall (a favourite spot for them in the Wet) no snake was to be seen — only an inert bright-green tree-frog looking like a plastic ornament at rest on the seat in one, and a lively gecko that ran over the wall in the other.

After rain the frogs rejoiced in a wide range of croaking tones. Some of the amphibians were quite large and had attractive markings; on another occasion, the young man with the baby croc had unexpectedly produced at the dinner table a huge brown-and-white frog, which was surprisingly slimy to touch. But of all the frogs I encountered, my favourite was an enormous splendid tree-frog which Albert had found sitting on a machine in the powerhouse. Some herpetologists who had just left the area had asked us to look out for this recently discovered species, and, if we caught any, to place them in spirit and send them to the University of Adelaide for study. Nobody had the heart to pickle the endearing yellow-spotted green creature from the powerhouse, so Martha happily gave it free run of her house.

Eventually the weather cleared and the sun blazed freely for long periods, though the sky was never devoid of clouds. Temperatures then soared to around 40°C, and after spending the first few hours of the day outside I would return to my air-conditioned room as grateful as any living creature seeking the coolness of a cave. As the sun spurred the growth of vegetation, canegrass seemed to spring up in front of my eyes, growing a good 10 centimetres a day; by the end of the season these grassy forests could well have reached heights of up to five metres. Wild-passionfruit vines, brightly decorated with flowers and fruits, scrambled along roadsides and the banks of streams. The ripe fruit tastes like the domestic variety, but is not as juicy; the unripe fruit and leaves are toxic if eaten in large quantities.

Every afternoon I visited the top lookout over the dam, the best place to watch the late afternoon's dramatic skyscapes. On most afternoons there was a buildup of monstrous cottonwool castles in the sky, ever-changing as they towered and swelled out to tremendous heights. Gradually the dazzling white of these clouds altered to angry shades of grey-blue and black; and often, before the rain fell, the rocks also turned to strange hues of dull orange, purple and chocolate.

Occasionally a storm unleashed its fury over the village. On my last afternoon I was nearly caught in one. I was out photographing some low-growing grevilleas and was so absorbed that I hadn't noticed an unusually heavy buildup of clouds. It wasn't until a sudden wind whipped the blooms that I glanced up at the sky, and after one look I couldn't race back to the village fast enough. I had been hoping to experience a good storm, but it would be better to be indoors for it! Just as I drove in, the rain started, and it was as if the taps of heaven had suddenly been turned full on. The grey curtains of rain that fell from the sky completely shrouded the ranges, the lake, and even the buildings close by. Waterfalls gushed over the rooftops and thunder rumbled steadily like booming cannons over the village. Generally rain is of little more than nuisance value to tourists, but monsoonal rain is fascinating to experience if you are not used to it. I took the opportunity to stand outside and wash my hair in the sheetlike downpour: this water from heaven was much softer than the very hard local riverwater. After an hour of dramatic entertainment the rain settled down to a steady downpour which lasted all night, flooding creeks and flattening areas of canegrass now lining the road like a high green fence. By midday the waters had receded and I managed to get through to Kununurra.

The few days I had in the town were not enough. Despite the heavy rain, the gravel road out to Hidden Valley was in good condition, and there was no problem getting there. It was an overcast day when Jack Roberts drove me out to the valley, and the warm colours of the freshly washed rocky walls looked magnificent against the vibrant green grass and the rockpools brimming with water. Later, from Kellys Knob Lookout above the town, the effect was that of a green blanket stretching before us over the Ord River plains. On a subsequent morning, the hill-country on the way to Wyndham looked splendid in its mantle of green, and the Grotto, situated close to the road, had water in it. Wyndham was *hot*. Other accessible and popular spots out of Kununurra were Valentine Springs, Black Rock Falls, and Dunham River Falls; most of the waterfalls in the district flow only after rain.

Recently I asked one woman involved in local tourism whether many visitors came to the Kimberley in the Wet — for I knew there had been a campaign down south to promote 'the green season'. 'To Broome, yes, but few come to the east Kimberley,' she said. 'The motorists won't come until the highway is an all-weather road right through the region.' Motorists may have to wait a while for that, but it probably won't be too long before more people come by air to see Kununurra in the green season; already an increasing number of overseas visitors are flying out to Home Valley at this time of year.

As I flew south after experiencing the Wet, I reflected on the past few exciting weeks. The most striking feature was the amazing fecundity of the land, and its ability to transform itself from a scene that was dry and tired-looking to one that pulsated with new life and freshness. Beautiful as the landscape was during the Dry, it was passive, as if part of its character lay dormant, waiting only for the monsoonal rains to roll in over the land to awaken it. Some northerners love this season, and say that if it wasn't for the Wet they would live elsewhere. If I lived in the Kimberley, I'm sure I would feel the same way.

Hidden Valley in the wet season

The Ord River in spate flows swiftly over the causeway at Ivanhoe Crossing, 12 kilometres from Kununurra.

Splendid tree-frog (*Litoria splendida*), one of Australia's largest frogs.

Facing page:

Lake Argyle and the Carr Boyd Range. In the foreground tall canegrass is growing.

Short-eared rock-wallaby among the boulders at the wall of the Ord Dam.

Wild passionfruit (*Passiflora foetida*). This is an introduced plant from South America.

THE RAINBIRD

Tonight I hear the rainbird calling,
calling
through the falling rain . . .
half asleep and half awake
I hear
a sound so lonely,
I fear
my heart will break.
For I can hear the rainbird calling,
calling
through the falling rain.

Still half awake and half asleep,
I keep
remembering the rainbird . . .
remembering his haunting call
and all
the long and lonely nights
when neither he nor I could
sleep.
And now I weep,
not only
for the rainbird . . .

NEROLI ROBERTS